Love Letters to Our Daughters

A Collection of Womanly Affirmations

Edited by

Angel C. Dye

For every brown girl who needs to know she is loved—may you draw strength, courage, and wisdom from the expressions on these pages.

For Maya, Zora, Alice, Nikki, Lucille, Toni, Edwidge, Octavia, and all of the literary giants who have helped me to fall in love with the written word. I am standing on your shoulders with hopes of being great.

Lastly, for Dr. S. Morgan. You are divinity, and I am honored to live in a world where people like you exist.

CONTENTS

Risks | Elmina Bell
A Dream Maybe | Nneka Azikiwe
Opportunities | Ms. RanaDee
If Summer Were a Person | Renée Walter
Parsecs Sounds Like Parsnips | Victoria Haviland

| On Love & Relationships |

Metamorphoses | Victoria Haviland
The ONE | Katherine Taylor
Love Blooms | Susan Miele
Love Personified | Queen Majeeda
Kings & Queens | Angel C. Dye
When You Entered My Broken Heart | E.
Naïve Love | E.
Pain Drives You | E.
Dear Journal | J.
Whole | Angel C. Dye
Soft Pastel Study | Victoria Haviland

| On Strength |

Flowers | Chelsee Self & Renée Walter
Wrong and Right | Sharon Cobb
Compliments | Angela Dye
Still Standing | Sharon Cobb
Inspire | Spencer Stultz
Be Yourself | Angela Dye
Try Again | Jacqulyn Washington
Anything Is Possible | Naketta Veals
Yes We Can | Aisha Gasle
Trying to Make It | Valerie Onifade
Based on a True Story | Angel C. Dye
Sis | Taylur Holland

| On Wisdom |

Flowers II | Angel C. Dye
Universal Law | Destiny Casson
Dear Journal | A.
QUEEN | Cyd Ahlberg
Beautiful You Are | Queen Majeeda
Don't Stop Dreaming | Janae Small
Advice to a Tumblr Friend | Elmina Bell
You Are Greatness | @iamsimplynay

ACKNOWLEDGMENTS

Embarking on the journey to compile these words, thoughts, and affirmations was healing. Seeing a vision given to me by God come to life in this work has helped me and strengthened me in ways that I do not have the words to describe. Many of the quotes within this work are from conversations I had with friends and family members over the last year. They did not even realize that they were helping me to fulfill my destiny to change lives until I would stop and say, "WOW. May I put that in my anthology?!" And they gladly obliged. I could not have done it without them.

I have so many people to thank for their contributions to this project. The first person I shared this vision with was my mother. She encouraged me from the beginning to see it through and to trust God to complete the "good work" he had begun in me (Philippians 1:6). Alongside her prayers she offered her own words to be shared here, her ongoing love and support, and her wallet! Mommy, I'm eternally grateful. My surrogate mothers who shared words here, I thank you. Aunts, cousins, sisters, friends, thank you. To anyone who in any way supported the coming together of this project…thank you. Your encouragement, your donations, and your love are what made the fulfillment of this book possible.

A very special thanks to supporters Susan M., Justus R., Anja S., Caroline C., Yinka A., Karsyn C., Samara R., Chrycka H., RebeKah H., Lakeisha R., A.L., S.B., J.M., S.C., R.I., A.J.C., and T.H. for your financial contributions to this vision!

Finally, Jesus, my Father, you have held onto me when I tried to let you go so many times. My natural fears sometimes discouraged me spiritually from doing what I knew you called me to do. Still I thank you for gifting me and gracing me through this process and this season, and I am excited to follow where you lead me forward from here. I pray that these words will uplift, inspire, encourage, motivate, and change lives just as you intend for them to.

WOMANIST

1. From *womanish*. (Opp. of "girlish," i.e. frivolous, irresponsible, not serious.) A black feminist or feminist of color. From the black folk expression of mothers to female children, "you acting womanish," i.e., like a woman. Usually referring to outrageous, audacious, courageous or *willful* behavior. Wanting to know more and in greater depth than is considered "good" for one. Interested in grown up doings. Acting grown up. Being grown up. Interchangeable with another black folk expression: "You trying to be grown." Responsible. In charge. *Serious.*

2. *Also:* A woman who loves other women, sexually and/or nonsexually. Appreciates and prefers women's culture, women's emotional flexibility (values tears as natural counterbalance of laughter), and women's strength. Sometimes loves individual men, sexually and/or nonsexually. Committed to survival and wholeness of entire people, male *and* female. Not a separatist, except periodically, for health. Traditionally a universalist, as in: "Mama, why are we brown, pink, and yellow, and our cousins are white, beige and black?" Ans. "Well, you know the colored race is just like a flower garden, with every color flower represented." Traditionally capable, as in: "Mama, I'm walking to Canada and I'm taking you and a bunch of other slaves with me." Reply: "It wouldn't be the first time."

3. Loves music. Loves dance. Loves the moon. *Loves* the Spirit. Loves love and food and roundness. Loves struggle. *Loves* the Folk. Loves herself. *Regardless.*

4. Womanist is to feminist as purple is to lavender.

From Alice Walker's *In Search of Our Mothers' Gardens: Womanist Prose* © 1983.

LOVE LETTERS
TO
OUR DAUGHTERS

#LLTOD #LLTOD #LLTOD
#LLTOD #LLTOD #LLTOD
#LLTOD #LLTOD #LLTOD
#LLTOD #LLTOD #LLTOD
#LLTOD #LLTOD #LLTOD
#LLTOD #LLTOD #LLTOD
#LLTOD #LLTOD #LLTOD
#LLTOD #LLTOD #LLTOD
#LLTOD #LLTOD #LLTOD
#LLTOD #LLTOD #LLTOD

Shekinah Hockenhull

Dear Us,

We are called many things. She, her, them, girl, woman, queen, daughter, sister, friend, lover, wife, baby, sweetie, honey, dear. But this…this offering is about who we are. The names we are given are not always the ones we answer to or the ones that really reveal our identity, but they are parts of us nevertheless. This is really a book of names, names we were given, names we chose, and names we are still discovering.

See, we are art and artists simultaneously. I read Alice Walker's *In Search of Our Mothers' Gardens* through a narrowly historical lens as a college freshman. Retrospectively, when my own mother sent me a beautiful poem for this book now two years later I finally get it. I never thought of her as an artist or a creator (besides the beautiful, albeit tumultuous, situation in which she created me). I never considered her working jobs she only tolerated for the sake of our survival or paying parts of bills and floating others so I wouldn't read eviction notices like scriptures *art*.

But our existence is art. Our breath, blood, tears…even our fears and anxieties are masterpieces. There is no one way to be woman. There is no bone and flesh prototype of femininity, and if the elders and ancestors have willed anything to us it is the opportunity to be our unabashed selves in the ways that they were not able to. It is the chance to make a kamikaze palette of the monolithic cesspool we are thought and expected to be. Most of the women represented in this work are not writers, per se. They do not call themselves poets, artists, or experts on anything. Still, their willingness to share their voices and vulnerability here makes them beautiful griots—storytellers.

"Queen" is written so many times throughout these pages. When you see it think of yourself, but understand it too. A queen is the highest woman in the land. A supreme being. A mother to nations. An heiress to royalty. She is worthy. We are worthy.

Answer to any names you want or don't answer to any at all, but do it the way you want to do it because you want to do it. Maybe you'll find some new names you never knew could apply to you. And yes. I said "us." This applies to her, her, you, and me too.

Yours in feminine solidarity,

Angel

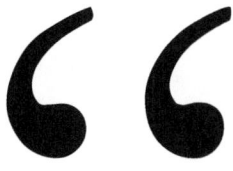 I have to create or I'll

suffocate."

— Ericka Jeanvil

| On Self-Discovery |

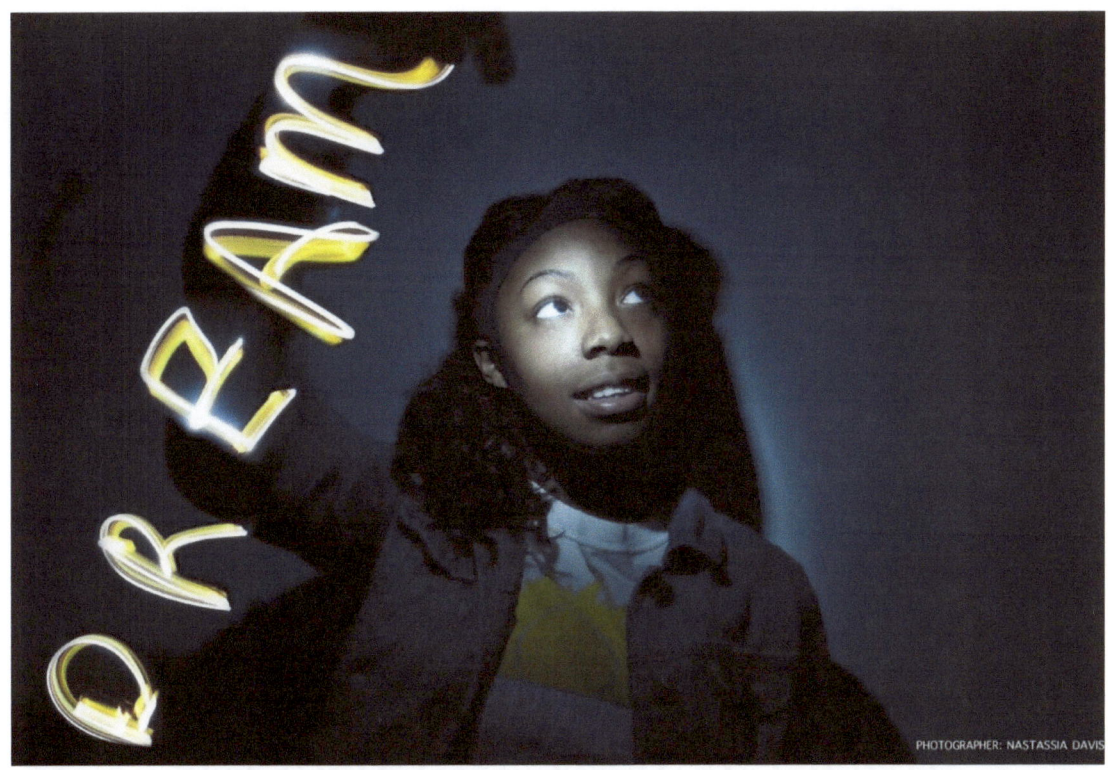

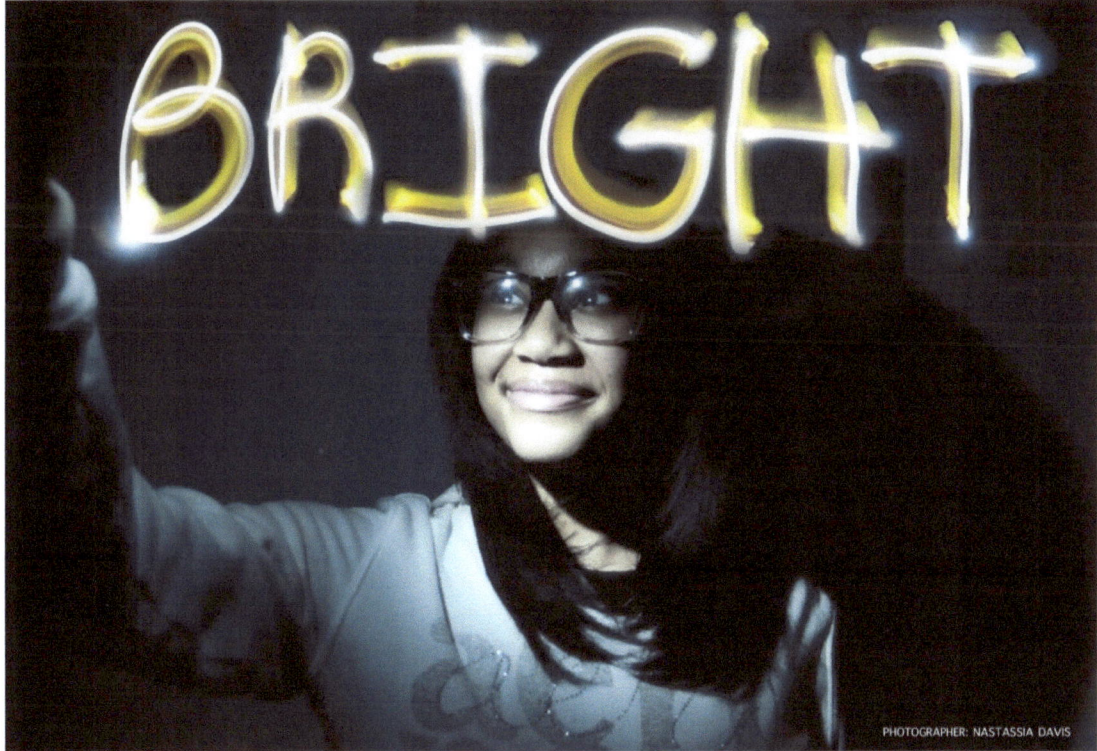

Dream & Bright | Fine Art Photographer, Nastassia Davis - http://nastassiadavis.com

" The wonderful thing about being a woman is that I am, by definition, a mystery—a puzzle that cannot easily be put together."

— Angel C. Dye

Identity | Taylur Holland

My identity is founded upon the words that You spoke.

Long ago, before the beginning of time, You were. And You gave me a name.

You named me and gave me a purpose.

You planned my course and wrote my story.

Everyday, I live out these words
And move closer and closer to destiny.

There are conditions and there are delays, but Your words are infallible.

I make mistakes, but I've been graced with Your identity.

In Your image, I was formed,
And into sin I was born,
But who I am has not been made null and void.

My spirit and my flesh are in constant antagony,
Warring to the point of unrest.

But still, I am a word that passed through flawless lips.

Still, I am a child, a king, a daughter of the Most High, for I came from Wonder and Delight.

That is my identity.

That is who I am–a word founded upon authority, power, and majesty–

A word that was spoken from the core of a flawless heart–

A word that came from Greatness Himself. Oh how I am in awe that He even takes thought of me!

I am a manifestation of His word–words that have been settled in heaven for ages–even before Time learned its name and proper place.

I am seated in heavenly places, amongst stars that have been counted as righteous through faith in Him who came to show me who I am.

What a reflection–what a matchless image…Oh how I've been graced to look just like Him!

I am a word made manifest here in the earth,

A word that will return to Him—but not without first accomplishing what He set out for me to do…for it is all for His eternal glory and purpose.

I am a word that will not return to Him void.

That is my identity.

> " I found it hard to love myself because being a dark-skinned girl was not seen as pretty or beautiful. I hope this poem will encourage our daughters to look deeper than skin and realize that beauty comes from within."
>
> – Melle Tibe

Pretty
You're so pretty for a dark-skinned girl
You're such a pretty black
Yes, you're a sexy black
Pretty
You're so pretty for a dark-skinned girl

Well how pretty am I really?
Or are you just that ugly...to assume my physical appearance defines my pretty.

"Broken men, you do not own me.

You did not breathe life into this body,

and you sure won't take the life out of it."

— Renée Walter

"Stop!" I said. "Leave me alone! You are hurting me!"

As tears started rolling down my face he pushed my head down into the couch saying, "So you are going to leave? You want that other nigga? Does he treat you better than I do? Well fine! Go get him!"

As I rushed to the door I was tripped by a size 14 shoe. As I reached the door my body was slammed against the wall hitting my head against a picture frame as the tears began to flow even more.

"I loved you liked no one else did," said this tall black man. He began to choke me until I was almost unconscious. I pushed him back then I kicked him in his genitals. I broke away from the chokehold, ran to my car, started the ignition, and drove off. My misery was behind, and my future was ahead.

I now stand free from what I thought love really was. Now I see love daily from my Heavenly Father. He graces me with life every morning I wake. My sister, you can make it! Set yourself free like the mother bird does her child. Fly high above and soar. The race is not given to the swift or the strong, but it's given to the one who endures to the end.

I'm free,

E. Mil

girl child | Angel C. Dye

what if i hadn't been born a girl child?
all round-faced and brown-eyed,
soft-skinned and hair-bowed
what if i could have bypassed the divide between wearing skirts and chasing them,
placing too much value on my looks and giving girls complexes about theirs
what would it have been like getting a pat on the back just for being born with an
anatomical advantage?
carrying nations under my slacks and the power to throne or dethrone queens by
loving them or just hitting it from the back
no one questions a man's strength
he is, after all, a man
he can basketball/football/track scholarship his way to corporate success, and our
two degrees will equal more pay for him even though i am the one holding down a
career, a social life, and a family
his pain will be invalidated because of his masculinity. 'men don't get raped. they do
the raping.'
mine somehow becomes my own fault. 'well what were you wearing when…'
i was wearing shame because my body causes offense by virtue of existence
i was wearing confusion because my mind is ironically an afterthought in the grand
scheme of me
i was wearing what-ifs and maybes because my mom once said she wanted a
son…already had his name picked out
and deep down don't all fathers want sons too?
i cannot be a lifelong apology. i was born a girl child by no divine doings of my own,
and i am proud.
proud skin and bones and womb and heart and soul and mind
proud girl child

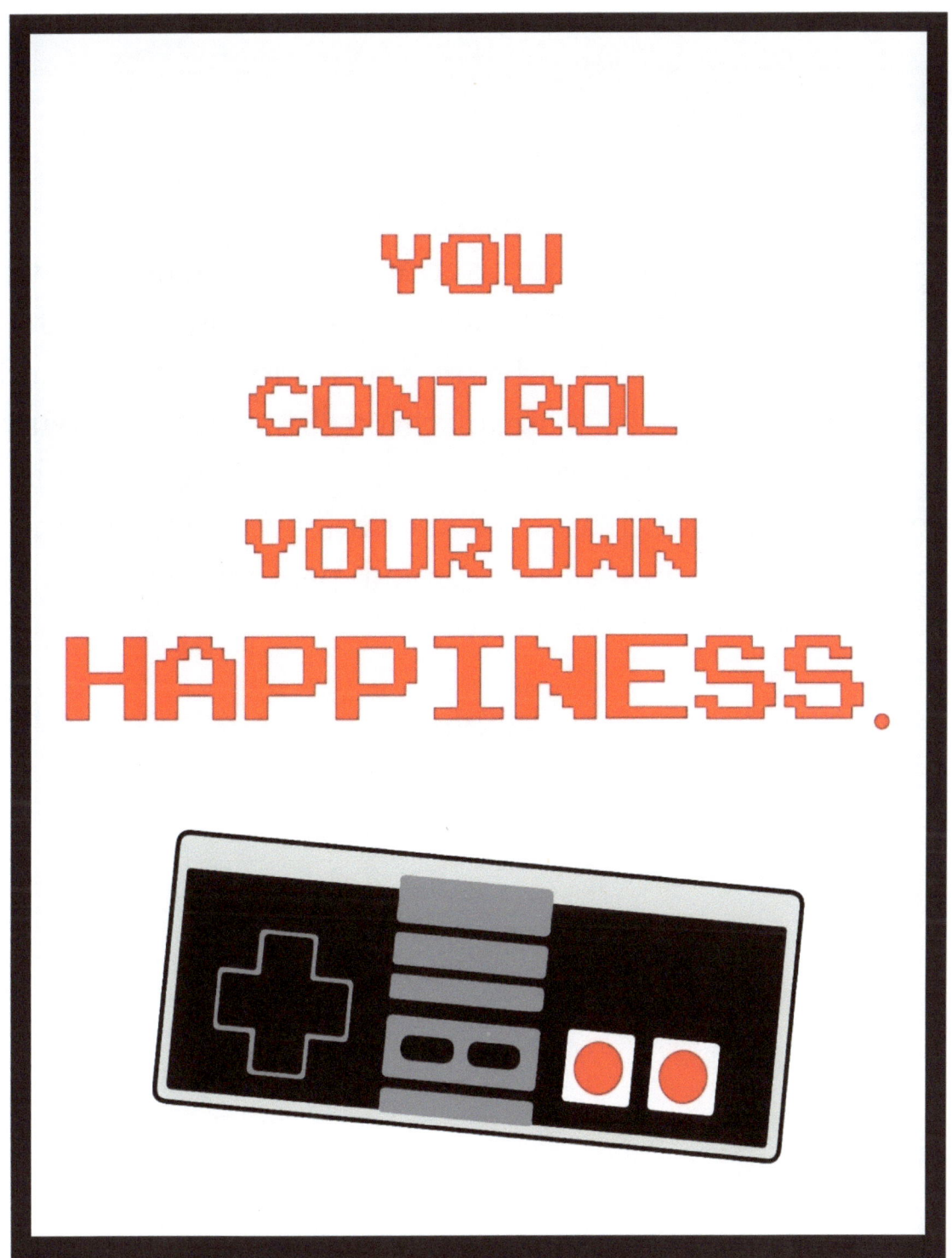

| Cyd Ahlberg |

" There is an inner beauty about a woman who believes in herself, who knows she is capable of anything that she puts her mind to. There is a beauty in the strength and determination of a woman who follows her own path, who isn't thrown off by obstacles along the way. There is a beauty about a woman whose confidence comes from experiences, who knows she can fall, pick herself up, and move on."

— Niké

Daughter | Savannah Bowen

Pregnant skies
Groan and quiver
Electricity strikes
Swelling belly and breast
Water breaks
And the cry of a
New dawn
Tears apart the
Stretching ceiling
Make way for the sun!
Make way for the hopeful morning!
From the darkness of a womb,
From a night of weeping,
A daughter is born.

Invisible Girl | Chrycka Harper

Dear Invisible Girl,

You are not invisible

You carry yourself as an inferior.

You blame your lack of confidence on invisible forces.

Kept blaming your weirdness, as if it were a disease.

So for one moment I ask you to trust me and

Be a Queen of the Night.

Take off your clothes. Seduce yourself. Hum a tune if you have to.

Gaze at the body that carries a feminine legacy of vitality, passion, and wit.

Release the memories of people calling you weird, awkward, and quiet for a Black girl.

This is the moment where you slowly fall in love with yourself.

It starts as a teasing pull at the corner of your lips.

Then it spreads to the point where your body bounces in joy.

You are not invisible. You are indeed beautiful.

Be a Queen of the Night

Sincerely,

Your Queen to Be

Harvest | Savannah Bowen

If you love me you will know me
You will show me that you can
Blow new life into
Yellow-green souls
With just one breath,
That you can sow me
Like new crop
And I will rise up,
My roots drinking love as it runs
Like water from the skies above.
I will reach with green branches towards
My hope, the warmth of your sun.
You will find me supple and strong.
Although slowly, you will grow me
to be the harvest
of a ripe and plentiful season
And my life will be bread for the starving people.

" When you find the thing that you love to do you have to do it."

— Angel C. Dye

Dance Skeleton | Ava Robinson

Paralysis.

The word, the condition,

frightens my soul and weakens my bones

down to the flesh, locating the muscles,

blood vessels, tissue and cartilage

until there is nothing left.

Not a ligament torn to cause a sprain.

Not an overstretched tendon to cause a strain.

No worries, no cares.

As my feet explore the floor

tension is released.

Expression is the key that

unlocks the beast in me.

My soul is held hostage against my will in the closet.

Thrilled by the sound of wire hangers, in the nude,

they dance, like chimes in the wind.

Magically sending chills up my spine.

Two oh six, Two hundred and six,

number embodies the abundance of my body image.

The framework, the fear of being internally fractured.

Broken pieces of a puzzle, scrambled,

ask to be put back together for the sake of the life,

lifestyle of a dancer.

Grandma and mama
smile
when you cry about a woman's cross
they all carry the scars and trials on their temple
yet when they turn their face
a strength that lifetimes have yet to test
oh, they'll never fail to reach out
with a cool embrace
for your hot and heavy heart
always murmuring, *honey you ain't seen nothing yet*

| Valerie Onifade |

Little Girl Blue | Raina McKinley

Little Girl Blue

swings from branches and climbs on rocks, her dirt-covered sneakers barely clinging to her feet by their velcro.

She ignores her mother's protests as she heads straight to the little boys' aisle.

Her hands, tiny as they are, are already calloused from

playing a bit too rough; she'd rather ride bikes with the boys than play tea party with the girls.

At night when she's alone in her room she'll play dress

up, her pants sagging, how she'd seen her cousin do, her

hat tilted backwards just as he'd worn his.

When she's done she'll sit down and secretly play with her

dolls, eventually, accidentally, beginning to play as the Dad.

And maybe one day while her friends are gawking at some boy, she'll be spending a tad too much time focused on Emily,

unsure if what she's feeling is jealousy or awe at the femininity she seems to so effortlessly produce.

She will try to mimic the dresses and pearls, but she never

does feel quite so pretty.

Whatever this masculinity is, it lives inside of her. She can't scrub it off or drench it in rosy perfumes and polishes.

But she'll find that one day she'll accept it. She'll return to the men's clothing section with a vengeance, and perhaps

a brand new haircut.

She'll look in the mirror and come to see she is finally

pretty.

Not in pink as they told her she should.

She looks much better in Blue.

Wo(man) | Angel C. Dye

I'm tired of being a prefix to him.

Bout sick of having my existence defined by the parameters he sets.

And I won't sit down, won't shut up, won't be tame and ladylike about it anymore.

What is ladylike anyway?

Whatever this lady likes.

I'm tired of being taught how not to be overly sensual, tired of being told to cover up and subdue my natural vibrancy so I don't steal the shine from him.

Dim my brilliance for who? Not you.

Teach us how to hold our keys between our knuckles as we walk home at night,

gift us pepper spray to arm us against him and his might,

send us on our way with worried frowns and "be safe."

No, no, no.

Teach him how to respect me, value me,

and don't use "if she were your daughter" to deter him from wanting to rape.

"Boys will be boys" is not law or fact,

and I won't accept clichés or excuses on his behalf because he doesn't know how to act.

No amount of hormones or alpha male complexes can make me alter who I am for him.

He's not primitive or beyond self-control, so why should I stand for his aggression and pacify his need to feel superior to me by stroking a fragile ego?

I'm big like the sun, dynamic like the universe, and divine like the heavens.

He can't take that away, you see.

And I know you thought this poem was meant to bash him, but you're wrong...

it's just to uplift me.

| On Motherhood |

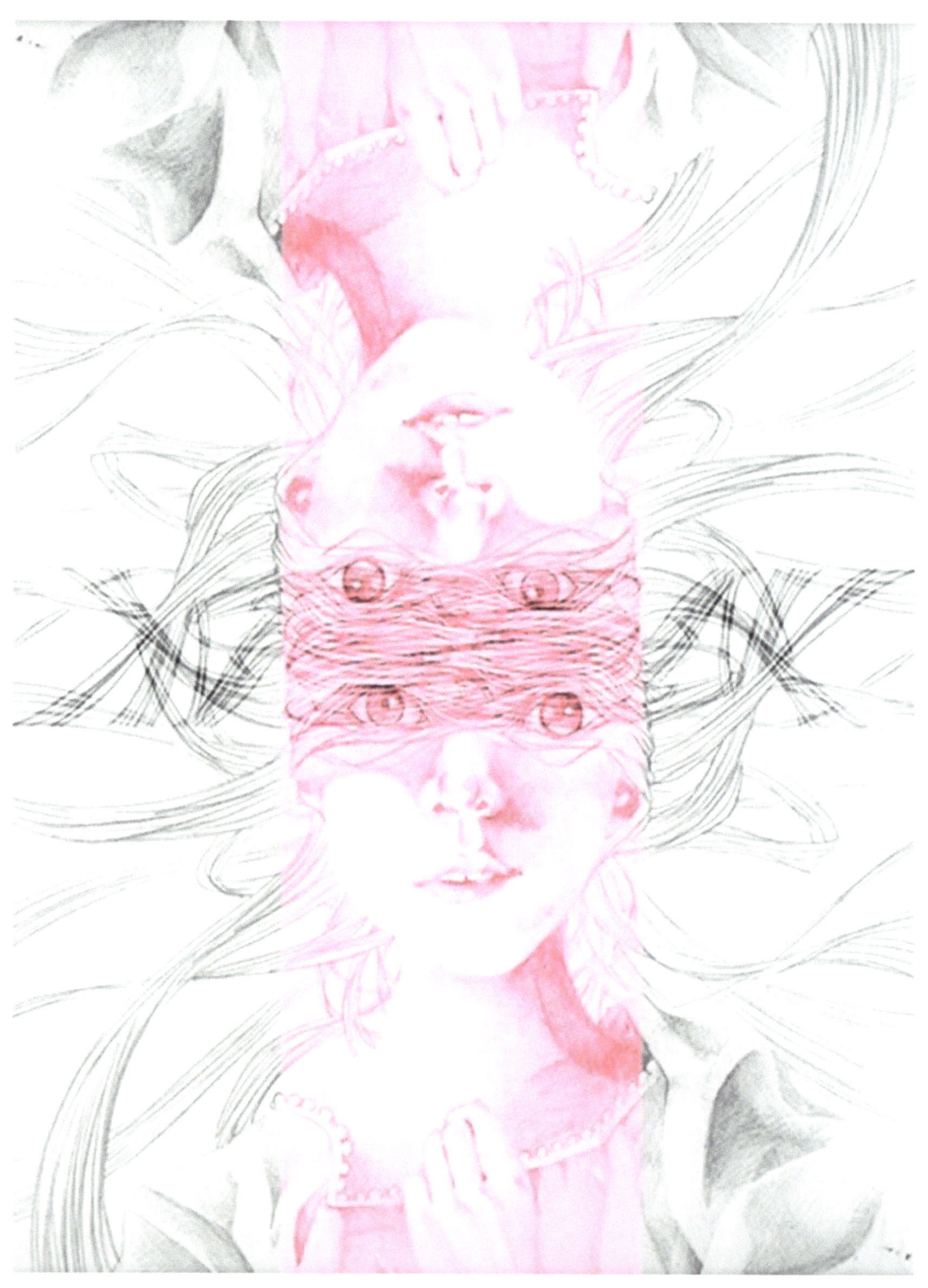

Reflection | Victoria Haviland

A Mother's Gift | Aisha Gasle

I first thought of the idea when I met a lady at my office.

She was dressed in a black dress, and a thin silver bracelet was dangling from her wrist. It was the only jewelry she wore, and it was certainly enough. There were a thousand dangly things attached to its many links.

I struck up a conversation with her and discovered that this was, in fact, a charm bracelet, and these were charms. Each charm stood for something.

The next week I found out I was pregnant, and I went out to buy you one. The only difference was that yours was gold.

You were born early at seven months, but you were a precious thing, your skin all pink and wrinkly from the womb. You hollered with all your might, and the sound was music to my ears because it told me you were alive. Your father, at my request, purchased a charm that looked like a musical note.

Over the years I added more. A silver tooth and a crawling child; the letter M, for your first word: *mommy*.

At age five, you decided you wanted to be a ballerina. I got you two sets of slippers: one for your feet, and one for your wrist. At age seven you switched to soccer. I added a soccer ball.

One day after school you returned home with a bloody nose and an enormous grin. You had fought a boy who insulted you—and won. I scolded you, but nonetheless, I felt that this deserved a marker as well. That week, you and I went shopping, and while you were browsing the doll section I bought a tiny sword on the sly.

You went from middle to high school, and I added a pencil. Your best friend hurt your feelings, and I bit back my sadness at seeing you in so much pain. That night I almost handed you the charm bracelet, but something made me take you out for ice cream instead. It wasn't ready although it was laden with little baubles and probably weighed a pound.

Finally, you graduated. Your father asked me while you were out with your friends just when I planned on giving you that gift. He convinced me that it was important because you were going off to college that fall, but I argued with myself and in the end I figured it was better to hang on to it.

"Admit it, Sarah," he scolded, "You don't want to let go of it. It's like an extension of her."

He was right. It held so much meaning for me by then and had been so much a part of you growing up. Handing it away, even though I had originally meant to, was going to be hard.

We were there for your college graduation, and as you received your diploma I pressed the small navy box to my heart and decided that now was the time.

But it wasn't.

Daughter, as we sit here surrounded by all of your friends and some of your family on your wedding night, I watch you in your golden gown and hold back tears.

Twenty five years ago, you weren't even alive. Just a notion, a mark on a drugstore pregnancy test. I didn't know what you were going to turn out to be. I didn't know how much it would hurt me to let you out of my life.

I draw you aside as the women chatter, and I hand you the box. Your eyebrows come together, and a small line forms, a trait you've had since you were young. My eyes water.

When you open it I can see a flash of confusion in your eyes. You pluck it from the satin pillow and hold it in the air, where it dangles.

"Ma, what's this?" You ask, your voice soft.

And I tell you. I tell you about the woman at the office, and the day you were born. I finger each charm individually as I recall each chapter of your life. The day you sang at the talent show. When you got your first all A's report card. Your first heartbreak, your first steps, your first gap-toothed smile.

I look up, and there are tears running down your cheeks.

"Why didn't you tell me sooner?" You ask, your lower lip trembling. "You had this all of these years?"

I was right—the bracelet does weigh more than a pound. We figure this out as I fasten it around your wrist, the gold iridescent against your smooth brown skin. Your hand looks exactly like mine, except for the ring. You belong to someone else now.

We walk back to the room where the party is still going, but we take our time because we're also stepping backwards on memory lane. You tell me how scared you were that day that I was going to yell at you for fighting, or that you had only gone into soccer because your friends were doing it too. You tear up again when you look at the bracelet, and my heart melts. This was the perfect time to give it away I realize. Because it's also the night when I'm giving *you* away.

My thoughts when you drive away in that silly green Beetle with a sign taped to the back and rice raining down on your heads, are peaceful, and it is with a calm but tearful smile that I kiss you goodbye.

Your father asks me when we're on *our* way home what I want to do. I don't answer at first.

"Take me to the mall tomorrow," I tell him as I stare out of the window, imagining you in that ridiculously decorated car. "I want to buy a charm bracelet."

"For goodness sake, *another* one?"

"I want one for me this time." I wink at him. "And maybe one for you too."

"No thanks!" Your father laughs, pulling onto the highway. He steps on the accelerator, and we are pulled into traffic.

We laugh and talk about you all the way home.

Dear Naomi,

If you're reading this then you must be of age for me to drop
this knowledge on you. As I write this advice to you and try
to summarize the many lessons I've learned in my 21 years
of life I hope that you take this and listen up. I want you to
always look at this and cherish the words of wisdom I am
giving to you. I want this to help you grow and develop into the
beautiful woman I know you will be. So first thing's first: always,
always put God first in everything that you do, and the rest
will follow. God is your best friend, and with Him all things
are possible. I hope that one day you will get to know Him for
yourself and that the two of you establish a strong relationship.
Next, let me tell you how much I love you. You are my sunshine,
my bundle of joy, my everything. I want you to know that I'll always
love you, and I hope that one day you too will experience true love.
I want you to love with your whole heart no matter how many
times you get burned. Love is a beautiful thing, and don't ever let
anyone make you feel any different about that. Additionally,
I want you to live your life to the fullest. I want you to dream big
and explore the world. Go after the things that you really want and
know that you can do anything that you put your mind to. Naomi,
you are a beautiful black princess who will one day be a beautiful
black queen. Know your worth, be confident, and hold on to your
morals no matter what you see or hear in this world. Carry yourself
with class, dignity, and most importantly with respect. Finally, know
that your mommy loves you, and I'll always be here for you no matter what.

Always & Forever,

Jasmin

To my momma muffin, my brownie bean, my shmoopie, honey bunches-oh-oats,

There are so many things that I want to say. Words upon words, topic after topic. But I've decided that today I'll just write you a short letter about the very beginning.

Let me tell you, though yes, you have heard some parts of it before. What I did, when almost five months in, was find out that my baby blessing was in fact a little girl. First, a quick interjection to say that I was supposed to have been able to find out this information during my previous appointment. You know why I couldn't? According to the sonogram technician you wouldn't open your legs enough to see the goods. Ayyyye! Let's keep on keeping on that way, huh? But I digress...

During that appointment I was nervous as nervous could be. I don't mean in any type of negative way whatsoever, just in the most excited sense. When she told me that she could tell, that she knew, I started tearing up immediately. Please believe it when they tell you that hormones kick you in the tail when you're pregnant. Add that to my normal emotional levels, and I was at Crying Capacity Level 5! She asked again if I was sure I wanted to know and my "YES!!!" landed on the last syllable as it rolled out of her mouth. So after laughing a moment, she didn't make me wait any longer and simply said, "I'm about 99% positive that you are having a girl." It took me two beats. One and two. I held my breath just about that long and burst into tears. As you know, I had chosen your name already and I started talking to you by name from that moment, right after finding out. It was a bit garbled with the sobbing, but I'm pretty sure you understood me just fine when I touched my stomach and said, "Hello Cienah, my sweet girl. I love you so very much."

That's when I realized. I saw that as much as I truly meant it when I said, "No, I don't care. I just want a healthy baby," that I still was ridiculously excited at the specific thought of having a little girl. That was what I'd always thought about as a little bit myself playing with my dolls. Your grandparents, they believed in only buying me dolls that were representative of us. Only black dolls. I would do their hair like mine with the click-clack ponytail holders and change their clothes, name them things that rhymed with my name, talk to them all day and night. I'd imagine that one day when I was older I could really be a mom to a beautiful, brown-skinned baby girl. Then that moment, your moment, came and everything I ever thought and felt, all those wonderful feelings and memories came back to me in a rush, filling my heart to bursting. It was one of the two absolute best and most perfect moments of my entire existence. There is no chance that will ever change.

Now the next part is more of what I tell you when I get all nostalgic about how big and old you are now. How I went immediately to the store upon leaving the appointment. How I purchased one light blue denim overall dress, one white long sleeved onesie with a matching denim collar, and one pair of size ridiculous (zero) sandals. I took that little outfit to the register feeling like I was glowing all over, with yet more tears on my face. The cashier offered me her congratulations with the biggest smile. Everyone that looked at me that day smiled. I tell you every single person who encountered me in my travels home gave me full-on grins.

I could ramble on and on about just those few hours alone. But why I chose that day to write about, what I want you to take from this, is that that glow was because of you. It was because of the feeling you put in my mind, my heart, my soul, my being. From the first second knowing you were with me, you have always made me so extremely happy. You have always made me feel full of so much love and positive emotion that it couldn't be contained. Right this very moment as I'm writing this to you it's through my tears. Good tears, great tears, the best tears. Though things may not be what we would like them to be as of now…you know that we have been having some trying times. But... BUT... I hope you've been hearing me when I've said it changes nothing. I will love you more than anything on Earth and beyond until the end of time and on to something yet to be discovered. Just like your favorite song I used to sing to you, you will remain my sunshine... and my reason. You are the most amazing of blessings, the most radiant of spirits, and you were given to me. I thank God, and I thank You.

Please know and forever remember that my baby girl.

Always,

Your Mom xox

Cali Gray-Cowans

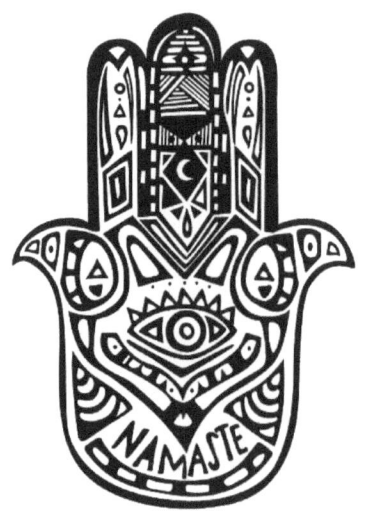

N
A
M
A
S
T
É

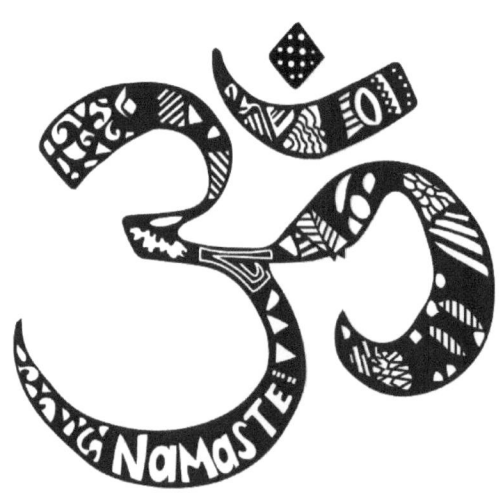

| Katherine Taylor |

December 2010

Ayana,

I just wanted to write you a note to thank you for your easy-going personality and heart full of love. I am <u>SO PROUD</u> of the woman you are becoming. I see you standing up more for what you believe in, taking care of your share of the burden since your stepfather died, and even correcting your sister when she's out of line, thus embracing your role as the big sister. This is a true mark of maturity. We've had a rough year as a family, but I've seen you ultimately trust in God and not be afraid to push ahead. You too should be proud of the miracles God is working in your life.

Thank you for supporting me, cheering me up, kissing me and hugging me too much, even when I am at times unlovable. :) Don't forget the quality you bring to any friendship or relationship. God will continue to protect and guide your life as you look forward to new and exciting adventures. I appreciate everything you do around the house.

Much love,

MOM

| Monica Carter to Ayana Taylor |

For my daughters, **Nehanda Sojourner** & **Thandiwe**: I've written these stories documenting your birth experience. They will remind you of your beginning, help you understand yourself, your strengths and weaknesses and gifts that will ultimately help you embrace your purpose in this life. Your life.

As the first-born child of my four children, you, *Nehanda*, have set the standard for my experiences as a mother. The ease of carrying you solidified my parenting style as you showed patience as a calm good-natured baby that provided me the confidence to do it again.

And my baby-girl twin, *Thandi*, as much as you insist that you are "the baby of the family," your provocative nature and humor never cease to blow me away with wisdom. It's clear that you will always lead in your very own way.

| Nehanda's Birth Story |

I had so many special experiences while carrying you. I knew without a doubt that you were a girl. I would constantly roll my eyes whenever Stan (Daddy) referred to you as an "*it*" or "*the baby.*" The act of carrying life, specifically *feminine life*, had me feeling super sharp, introspective and pensive, aware and extremely mindful of everything that came my way.

The most eye-opening, distressing, realization was the thought that my baby could be taken from me. And as much as I knew about the harrowing slave trade that brought our ancestors here it became very real to me on a level I hadn't imagined before. Learning about the rawness of slavery in high school (and not that surface stuff most of America thinks of) has always had an effect on my spirit and realization of the evils of mankind. But years later, becoming pregnant with you, Nehanda, made me wonder if I *had* experienced it and, maybe even, repressed it…This had me reconsider the merits of reincarnation or the idea that memories can be passed down…

So I could relate to Sethe, the protagonist in Toni Morrison's Pulitzer Prize winning novel, *Beloved*, who ran away with her two-year-old daughter and killed her rather than have her return to slavery. My obsessive thoughts about this subject probably opened a gateway that easily welcomed a very real spirit. I had a supernatural experience when I was barely three months pregnant with you, Nehanda. Stan and I went on a trip with my parents to tour several stops along the Underground Railroad in Missouri and Ohio.

Before going into this one particular location we were warned that it might feel distressing and heavy with sadness, that some of us might be disturbed and it was fine if we needed to exit. As soon as I entered I felt the heaviness and despair. After about five minutes inside I felt a strong feminine presence next to me as I stood away from the group, and I realized that I was being followed. I stopped immediately, relaxed and opened myself up, (physically and mentally) closed my eyes letting my arms fall to my side with my palms turned outward as you would to let a curious dog stop and sniff you. Trying to signal that I wasn't afraid, mostly worried that it would end or I'd scare her off some way. I was too curious to be afraid, and thankfully by that time I was quick to recognize what experiences were safe enough to pursue. It was definitely a "her," and I felt like she was sizing me up—looking me up and down, trying to figure *me* out, in search of something—and there was a reason she had chosen me and I wanted her to know I *welcomed* her presence.

We both stood there, like when two people bump into each other and realize they might be related but are not quite sure how…she was level to my height, face-to-face, our breathing pattern even but completely opposite of each other. I kept my mouth closed and breathed through my nose quietly but steadily. As she exhaled her breath fell on my face like humidity. She was scanning me like I was a long lost relative. After what seemed like several minutes she seemed satisfied and pleased. The humidity of her breath felt like a cool-down softly refreshing my face.

And then she was gone.

My eyes opened and the female tour guide grabbed me as I started to faint. She asked if I was okay then helped me outside for air. I told her everything, and she didn't express surprise but after I told her I was pregnant suggested that the Spirit must have sensed that I was carrying life and wanted to bestow a "blessing" on me, on us.

That evening I decided that Sojourner would be one of your names.

Later during my pregnancy I had visions. The most vivid of these were of my female ancestors standing on the ocean floor, standing on the shoulders of other women, miles deep into the ocean until the water covered the head of the woman at the top, everything but her hands jutting out above the water, holding a baby just above the surface. It humbled me, and I realized what a privilege it was to carry life! I said a prayer thanking the women in my bloodline who EXISTED so that *I* could live and exist for *you*.

And the dreams: I had one where there were several voices in a pitch black room, but a female child's voice did all the talking as these very old men waited for her wisdom. She was there to take questions from these very important men who waited impatiently to be advised by you so they could make decisions based on your advice. I was trying to see your face and asked if you were my daughter…but I knew you were. My womb represented "the darkness." After waking up from that dream I knew I was carrying some kind of wise person, a leader.

| Thandie's Baby Story |

Once upon a time, an anxious Nadine sat on her big red couch with a big quilting needle using the needle to separate 10 years' worth of loc'd hair. She was worried that something very wrong was happening with her body. She was fixated on this task because it gave her immediate satisfaction and a brief respite from worrying. Ever since she pulled that first loc apart at the back of her neck a few weeks back, she was obsessed with the thought of having her hair back and committed to getting them out however long it took.

After a week of sitting in the same position on the same couch, literally splitting hairs, she'd had enough stomach-clutching pains and decided to call her gynecologist. She was scheduled for an ultrasound the very next day. While sitting on her big red sofa she was resigned in the fact that her period wasn't coming. She'd made peace with the fact that she was pregnant, but this pain? That couldn't be good. Surely she was having a miscarriage. She was prepared either way.

She thought.

By the time she'd arrived at the technician's office she gave the oldest two children, ages six and one, snacks and made them comfortable in a corner far away from the examining table for privacy. She also asked the tech person not to speak loudly because of the kids. She didn't want them to be exposed to anything traumatic before she could process it herself.

The ultrasound had to be done with a wand inserted vaginally for accuracy and to pick up the smallest indication of life. Very weird with the kids a few feet away even though they had no idea what was happening. Nadine watched them eat granola bars and draw, and it calmed her thinking how cool it was that they had each other and how lucky she was to have a girl and a boy. As the technician began to work Nadine sat upright on the examining table watching the ultrasound screen show the image of her uterus. She kept glancing up at the stern-faced matronly technician while she focused on finding an image on the screen.

She held up two fingers. Nadine looked at her confused with a puzzled expression.

The technician mumbled in a strong Ukrainian accent, "Two."

"Two what?" Nadine replied.

"Babies…in there."

"Whaaaa..?"

"TWO BABIES?" she kept repeating while she dizzily lay back on the ultrasound table to process the words. The screen. The thought of TWO babies…

Soooo…no miscarriage? Not that she wanted one, but she had prepared herself to deal with a miscarriage. She did not expect to hear *those* words! Was all that pain caused by the babies attaching themselves to her uterus? How could that be so painful?

Weren't twins supposed to skip a generation?

She caught herself getting excited and looked over at the monitor to concentrate on the screen. She focused her gaze on an oblong dot about the size of a sesame seed flipping up and down frantically. And another, the same shape but a few inches away that appeared to be lying peacefully alongside the bottom of her uterus. She asked if those oblong shapes were the babies. When the tech lady confirmed, Nadine, without missing a beat, pointed to the sleeping zen-like shape the technician had since labeled "Baby A" and declared, "THAT is a boy and that…" (pointing to the flipping shape now reversing her direction but still flipping), "THAT is a girl."

She just knew and never thought for a second she was wrong. Never mind that at that stage it was way too early to be figuring out genders, but she just knew.

While she was finishing up the technician sensed that Nadine was still processing the info and made a point of saying, "You'll be okay. You're still young and strong."

Eight months later, Nadine's mother thought about carrying her own set of twins 36 years ago and smiled. "You're much stronger than I thought you were." Nadine was amused that her three sisters wanted twins but she got them instead. She was also proud that in addition to twins, her mother who also birthed 7 singletons, thought of her as strong. She smiled and wiped away a layer of perspiration. It was 96 degrees at noon and she shifted to reposition the babies, who, by now weighed over 12 pounds.

She was en route to her weekly appointment. Nadine would determine, based on baby-girl B's position if she would have a V-bac, or a vaginal birth after Cesarean, as her ambitious male doctor suggested. But Nadine already knew: baby-girl B was not traveling into the birth canal alongside her cooperative womb-mate anytime soon. Baby-girl B's feet were nestled in her favorite place, Nadine's ribcage. Kicking, happy, warm and comfy. C-section it would be.

— RebeKah Myatt Hammonds

| On Resilience |

" Sometimes you have to be at your lowest to create your best work or to be your strongest. It all comes full circle."

— Renée Walter

QUEEN TWEETS...

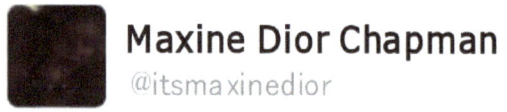 **Maxine Dior Chapman**
@itsmaxinedior

 Following

Vision. Ain't nothing in this world like a Black woman with one & the tenacity to make it manifest by any means necessary.

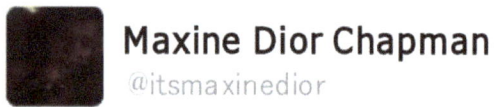 **Maxine Dior Chapman**
@itsmaxinedior

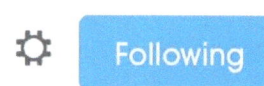 Following

#RaisingQueens. 👑

—— Maxine Chapman

"Nothing will ever happen if you don't take risks. 2014 taught me that. You have to get out of your comfort zone."

— Elmina Bell

A Dream Maybe | Nneka Azikiwe

Dizzy

Vision hazy

But not from the liquor

Eyes all glazy

Just high off life

A figure appears

And I think I know who

When I call out

Nothing.

When I scream out

Nothing.

Then I blink and my world returns

I'm still sitting on the curb

In the middle of a storm

I prefer the rain

To hide my pain

For nothing seems the same

In this life we call a game

As the rain continues to pour

I ask for nothing but an encore

To wash away the tears

Then out of the corner of my eye

Through the curtain of raindrops

A spark of light

A spark of life

A hint of the ending of the storm

A ray of sunshine

Hope

Happiness

I smile

I jump up

Everything seems just right

Ready to explore

Ready to embark

For the storm had passed me by

The troubles of my mind

Had seemed to settle for just a while

My emotions ran high

And I thought this world was mine

Mine for the keeping

Mine for the taking

And through my eyes

That figure reappeared

I shouted out

And I cried out

And the ground began to shake

The wind began to pick up

I could see the eyes of the figure

My head started to pound

The thunder started to roll

The figure began disappearing

And this moment of clarity

This moment of sunlight

This moment of life

This moment of calmness,

Was just the eye of the storm passing me by

My vision became blurry

The voices around me grew louder

And a familiar voice said

Wake up!

Wake up!

Wake up!

It was then that I realized

This storm that seemed so real

The figure that I knew

Was all just my thoughts gone astray

In this act I call a dream

" Opportunities don't make themselves."

— Ms. RanaDee

If Summer Were a Person | Renée Walter

If summer were a person she would be demanding.

She would beckon you outside with her bright smile and warm face
then drag you all around town, leaving you sweaty and burned out.
She would play with your hair and compliment your hat,
then she'd knocked it off and send you running down the street after it.
She would convince you to go for ice cream and then turn it into a
puddle of sticky soup before you could finish your sprinkles.

She would take you to the beach for a nice swim
and then roast you black—or red—leaving your skin too hot to touch.
She would make bus rides and train rides an absolute hell.
She would show you the Monarch butterflies and remind you that this was last time you would see
that particular batch alive.
She would make cold showers a lot more enjoyable.
She would warm your nights and annoyingly wake you with her blinding brightness.

If summer were a person she would give you peace.
She would remind you what nature feels like—the wind, the water, the grass.
She would remind you that bright days always follow dark nights.
She would remind you what childhood feels like.
She would show you what summer love feels like.
She would take you away from the city noise and the industrial air,
and she would remind you what it feels like to just...be.

Parsecs Sounds Like Parsnips | Victoria Haviland

The distance from our sun to our Earth
is 92,960,000 miles, which is 149,600,000 kilometers
(if we're trying to be inclusive), and that is a lot of time
to think about all of the times that I could have
talked to the boy who sat in front of me in my World
History class. Or how many fights I've gotten into
with my mother and what that must have felt

like for her. When I go to my family's cottage
on Crystal Lake I mostly look forward to the nighttime
because then I get to sit out on the porch with
my dad and my uncle and my cousins and we
look at the stars and swap space facts.
They're always surprised when I give out
the most. Like, it would take a bullet train 107.25 years

to get from Mars to Jupiter. Or that commercial space
travel is going to be possible in the near future
(which would be totally cool). Basically, when I think
about all of that void and everything that floats around
in it, when most people would feel insignificantly
small and unimportant, I feel amazed because I
am this nothing in vast nothingness and I matter, anyway.

| On Love & Relationships |

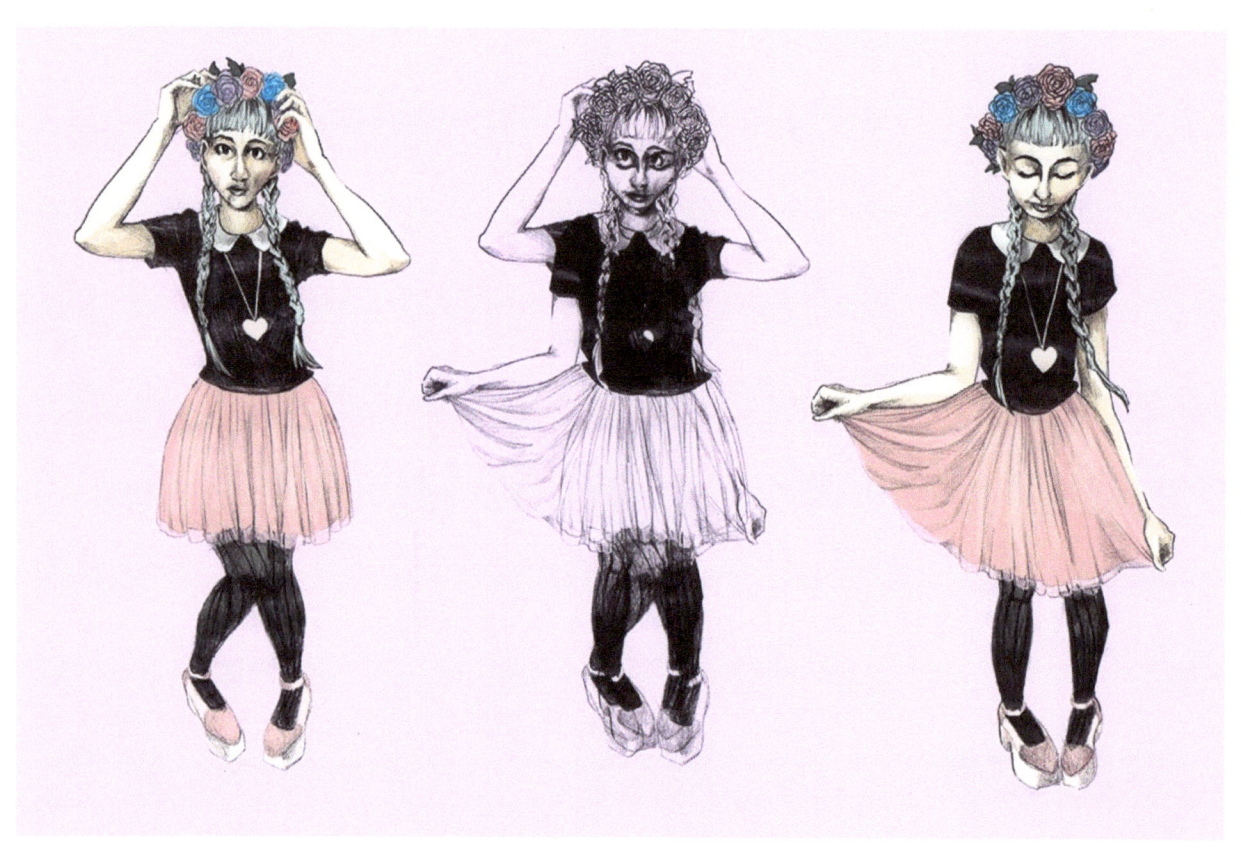

Metamorphoses | Victoria Haviland

On meeting *the one*…

"It'll happen out of nowhere, and it'll be amazing."

— Katherine Taylor

"So many young girls are afraid that they will never fall in love. If you want a person to notice you and really fall in love with you, do this: concentrate on improving yourself in any way you want. Learn things, go places, dance, love, laugh and allow yourself to make mistakes and act silly. If you feel anyone trying to curb your being comfortable doing these things move away from them. Do your best to surround yourself with love and acceptance. Those kinds of people will bring out the best in you, and you will inspire them to do the same.

Once you can do that people will notice you, watch you, try to be like you, and will be more comfortable being themselves. They will like to be near you. Lots of people will see your confidence and be attracted to it, but there will be one who is so very mesmerized by the light of your spirit that they will be unable to leave, and that is when love blooms."

— Susan Miele

Love Personified | Queen Majeeda

I turned to the mirror to gaze at my image
and wallow in self-pity
Because you love not only me but several others
Then why do I yearn for love,
when love is so cruel?

I sat down in front of the mirror
so that I could stare at myself and cry
But I beheld such beauty and I asked why?
Why should I cry?
And get those beautiful bright eyes
swollen and red?
Why should I get my face tear-stained,
to smear the coolness of my complexion?
I told myself no!
Being the aesthetic that I am
I hate to spoil true beauty
So I didn't cry
I thanked my Maker instead
For in the mirror I beheld
the beauty of His creation
I am love personified!

On what *he* can do to fulfill *her* in a relationship…

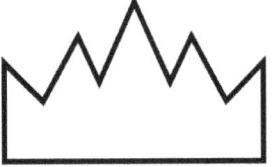

" He can crown me Queen by his existence as King."

— Angel C. Dye

WHEN YOU ENTERED MY BROKEN HEART

From the beginning, I had distanced myself from you—

scared.

But why? when your gaze felt so good and your attention so unreal and

Because I knew that if I got closer I would want more and it would bring pain

because girls like me don't get more; we usually get...

nothing.

But it was too late, I had already begun to feel some of the pieces of my heart coming back together

My craving for love and attention was strong but I concealed it...even from, myself.

what happened to my self-control

my ability to appear strong but in reality just hiding, hurting

what happened was my craving for love overrode my thoughts and value for myself

But I could not blame myself.

Not when my whole life I had survived with just crumbs off of the table and you were a whole loaf of bread.

— E

NAÏVE LOVE

Being with you
was like
the feeling a six year old gets when they have a piece of candy
but deeper, worse.
Because by the time a child is six, they have probably already had pieces of
candy
And me,
well I had barely had a bite
So of course the candy is ten times sweeter
I craved it ten times more, your attention and affection
because not only did I think I would never have it,
I did not know how good it would taste.

— E

PAIN DRIVES YOU

i held in the pain because i was in pain

but i had to let it out cuz it was driving me insane
how much hurt can a heart hold

my heart was so filled with hurt and it led to my feelings being told,

spilling everywhere, that pain.

and there was no rag to wipe it so it left many stains

— E

Dear Journal,

Why are boys so stupid? Like really...what is it that goes through their minds, I wonder? The stuff that comes out of their mouths sometimes leaves me like -__-. For example, I was walking from my job to go get some food for dinner just a few minutes ago and I overheard these two boys having a conversation about a girl. It was the usual...one of the boys trying to have sex with some girl, and he was telling his friend about his *pursuit*. From what I gathered the girl is/was a virgin and wasn't trying to let anyone know she did/was thinking about losing her virginity to him. Kind of like a "If we do this do you promise not to tell anyone?" (i.e. "Don't tell ya homeboys.") This is the problem with eavesdropping (unintentionally in my case): I don't really know the whole story. I'm just getting bits and pieces because I'm actually trying to mind my business, but the story is rather interesting.

Anywho, back to the conversation. The boy's friend was like, "Bruh, she's a virgin?! Like a virgin *virgin*?" -_____- I get what he was trying to ask, but it just sounded dumb. He was basically asking whether or not she has refrained from participating in ANY type of sexual activity besides the obvious abstinence of having sex. The friend then laughed when the guy was like, "Yeah, she hasn't done anything, man." Again, I admit I don't know the backstory, but a few things stood out to me in this brief eavesdropping session: 1. Why was it funny that she was a virgin? 2. Why are you trying to put her on blast if she's coming to you about losing her virginity (if this is the situation)? Now, we all know that you're supposed to wait until you're married to engage in sexual relations. You're supposed to save yourself for your husband because the act bonds the two individuals as one, and that's what makes it sacred—we got that. We also know that the no one is perfect. We're all sinners. No matter what sin we commit they're all weighed the same, and we sometimes get tempted by the devil and fail God—we got that too. And maybe this girl is/has been tempted and has given in, BUT if she hasn't then I hope she doesn't because this man is not deserving of such an intimate act. Not even close, bruh. Not even a maybe.

At that point I was so disgusted because this always happens. This society is TOO focused on sex like they can't possibly wait or hold out. This society/generation, whatever you want to categorize it as, treats sex as if it's not sacred anymore because it's all over social media and people's phones and stuff, which is a shame. It's not that hard to be abstinent; you just have to choose not to give in. I chose not to give in for 20 years, son! Now alright, most of those years I was too young to understand what it REALLY was about but still. If you look at it from the perspective of "I didn't do it for 14, 16, 17, 20 years, etc. what's another 7, 8, or 9 honestly?" I gave in. I knew it was wrong, but I got caught up in emotions and *feeling good*. Remember that part I said about us all being sinners and that we all get tempted sometimes and fail? Yeah. I was talking about me too. Although I knew it was wrong I did it anyhow because I was doing what I wanted to do and not what God wanted me to do. Out here living for the world as if THEY hold my salvation...smh. But that's another story for another time.

Sometimes I can't believe I did that, but I take ownership of my actions. I'm done with that now, and if you don't think about sex constantly (as society often places emphasis on) then it's honestly not that difficult to remain a virgin/celibate. So when he laughed I didn't understand what was funny. Nevertheless, these types of conversations always occur among the "men" of my age group. Why does it have to be, "Guess who I smashed this weekend," or "I'm working on gettin' with her, but I'm not tryna be her man for real?" Again... -_____- Like why? For what reason is that even necessary? Is anyone genuine anymore?! Oh no, we're back at this phase again. I've felt this way my whole life basically…since the time I started liking boys and I saw how good girls get taken advantage of (emotionally) or get looked over because "they're too hard to get" (i.e. the story of my life). I wonder if boys ever grow up and mature. I mean I know they do EVENTUALLY. I can see that, but when you're in your 20's and trying to sift through it it's like #I'mNotHereForThis. Call me back when you're 30 and trying to settle down. I'll see if your resumé is worth taking a look at this time.

I don't know, man. Maybe it's because I'm wise beyond my years, but I'm just NOT here for the immaturity in certain aspects. I figure if I'm up to par then you can be up to par too, bruh. I know you're not supposed to be super serious all the time, and yeah, you may not have the urge to settle down at the moment…and that's cool! I'm not tryna get married and have kids by the next year either, buuuuutttt I DO expect you to not play games, yo. I DO expect you to know how to treat someone with respect whether you're involved with them for two weeks or two years. Be genuine, bruh. Be honest! Be monogamous, dang it! Lol. Is that too much to ask?! You can't narrow down what you want in a mate if you're talking to two or three girls, having sex with three or four girls, and seriously trying to get one because you think she's the one for the long haul. No, bruh, that's not how it works. I feel like when you're talking to someone you should only focus on that one, and no, not five or six months down the road. I would say two or three months into dating you should make a decision as to who you're going to commit to getting to know better and maybe build something with. If it doesn't work, okay then. Move on to the next. If it does then great. You're on the right track. It's not that hard, man…it's really not. But yeah, that's the end of my rant…lol. I had to get that out, yo. Boys just frustrate me sometimes. It's almost as if you want to knock some sense into them like, "When will you get it, bruh?!" But for real for real I gotta be out. I have to study and do my hair so on that note…peace.

—J

"I want to be *realized* and not idealized or objectified."

— Angel C. Dye

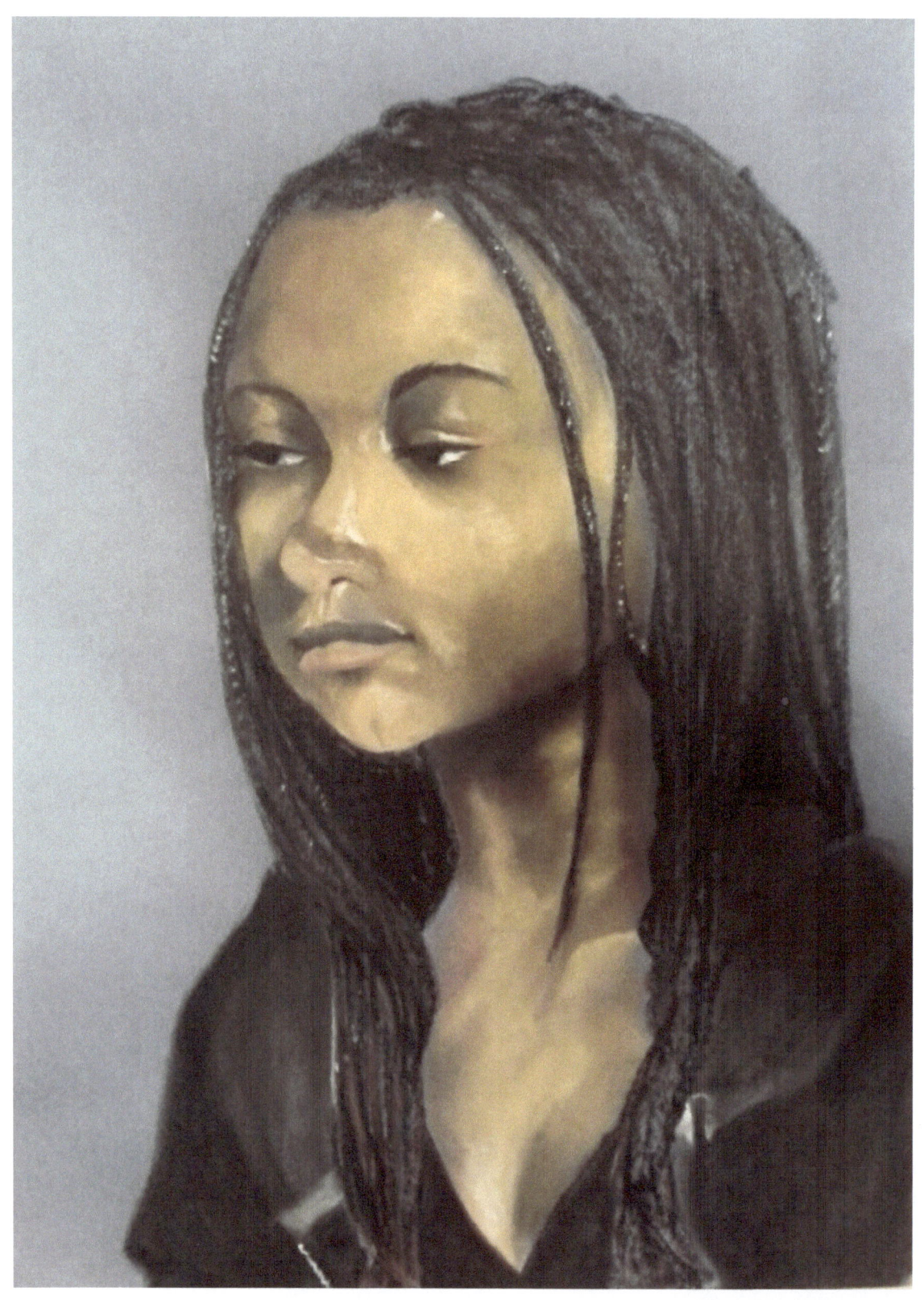

| Victoria Haviland |

| On Strength |

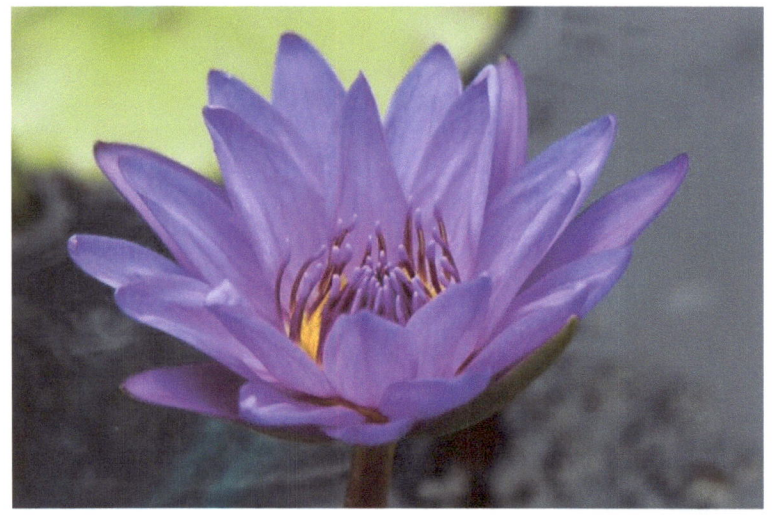

"Embrace the careers,

misplaced fears,

confidence, success,

and power.

And remember…

no one but you can
stand in your way,

so don't be a stone—

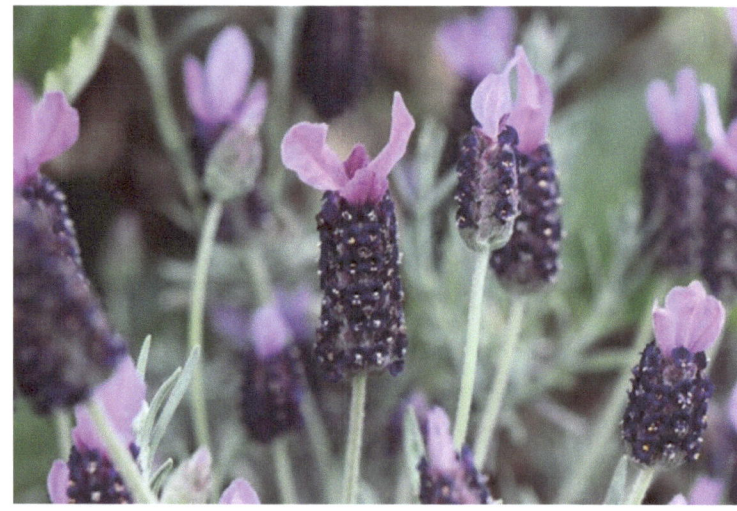

Be a flower."

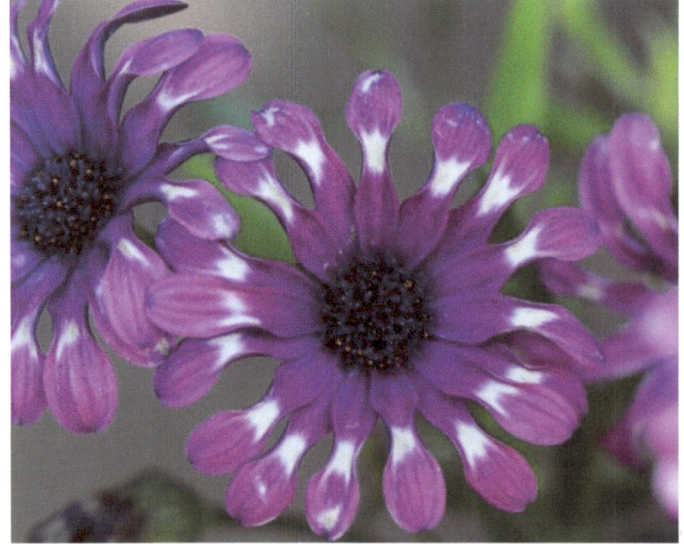

Photos by Chelsee Self, poem by Renée Walter

"For every person who does wrong in your life there is one who does right. Remember that."

— Sharon Cobb

" I don't allow compliments to amplify my head. Likewise, I don't allow negativity to make me feel reduced. It's how I feel about me, and I believe every being is EQUALLY beautiful. My *spirit* is what I seek to impress with. So if my looks are the only thing acknowledged *I'm* not impressed. Shallow minds are uninteresting."

— Angela Dye

Still Standing | Sharon Cobb

I have been through good times and bad times, but I am still standing.

I have had happy times and sad, but I am still standing.

I have had prosperous times and lean times, but I am still standing.

I have been knocked down with no way to get up, but I am still standing.

I have been lied on and talked about, but I am still standing.

I have been mistreated and abused, but I am still standing.

I have often been misunderstood, but I am still standing

I have had laugher and I have had tears, but I am still standing.

I have been sick and I could not get well, but I am still standing.

I have seen the light of day and I have seen the darkness of night, but I am still standing.

Though I have experienced much…thank GOD that I am still standing.

"You never know who you'll inspire just by doing you and just by doing good."

— Spencer Stultz

" When all is said and done you'll find your biggest competition is in yourself—to become that person who another fell in love with at the start…which is why you should always be yourself. That way you don't have much to remember."

— Angela Dye

" I've come to the conclusion that I'm the person keeping me from success. Every time I try to do something I get so afraid…but I'm going to try again."

— Jacqulyn Washington

" I have made mistakes in my life and learned from my mistakes. We all make mistakes; we just have to learn from them. Being a single mother is hard work, and there is never a day off. I would say to young girls get your education first and don't rush to grow up. Don't rush to have a child just because the person that you are with says that if you don't have a baby right away they are leaving. You should let them leave because if they really love you they will wait until you accomplish your goals before expecting you to have a child. For those single mothers and fathers who want to go to college or want to finish high school I encourage you to finish. Just because you have a child you don't have to put things on hold. It won't be easy going to school, working, and taking care of your child, but you are stronger than you think and with GOD anything is possible. I go to school, work, and take care of my child and yes, sometimes it's hard, but it makes me stronger and seeing my child's face motivates me."

— Naketta Veals

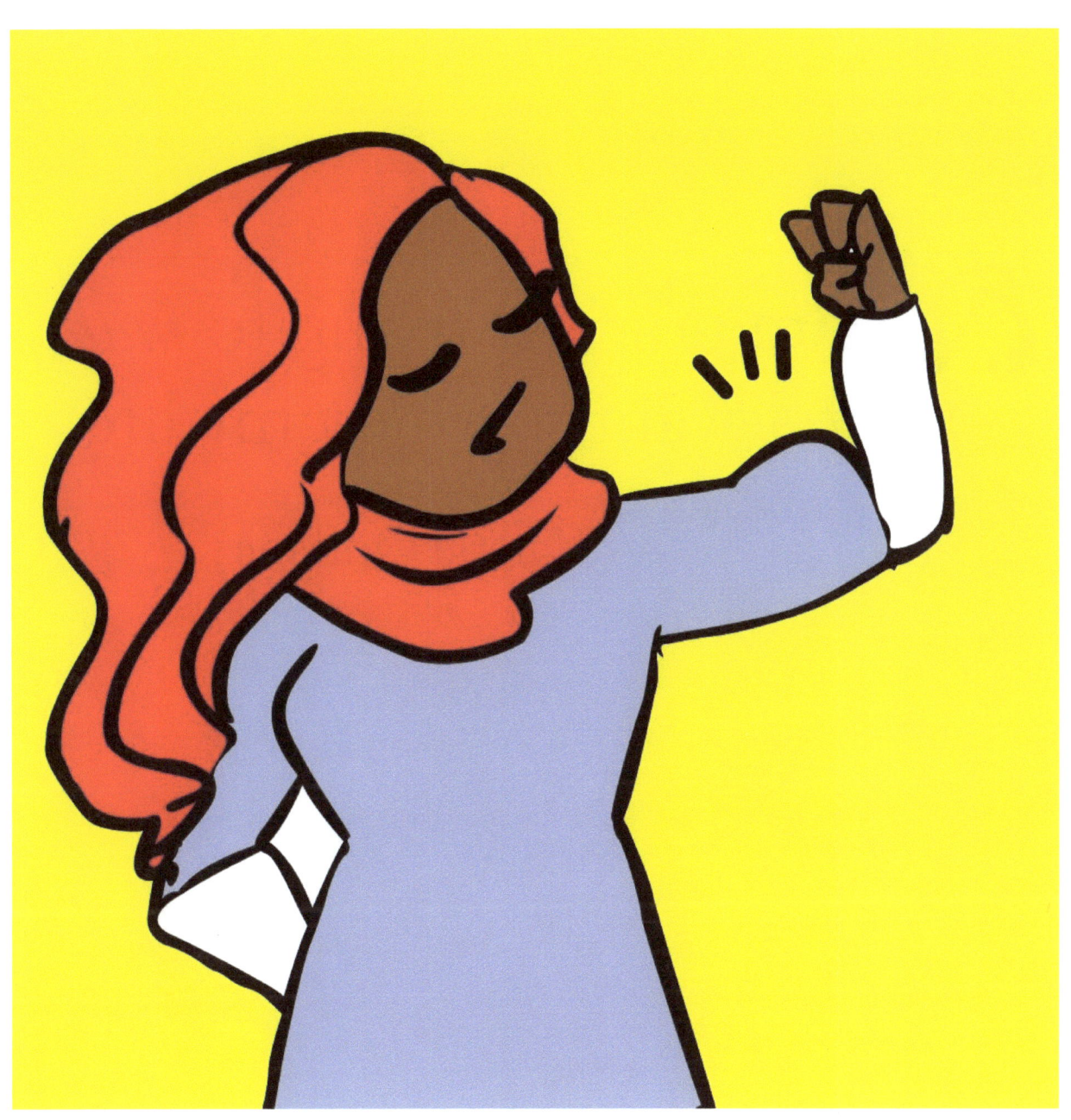

Yes We Can | Aisha Gasle

" I'm not just trying to *make it*. I want to enjoy my life."

— Valerie Onifade

Based on a True Story | Angel C. Dye

Tell the truth. Tell your
truth, and let it be enough.
Tell it, yell it—LOUD.

They hurt me, touched me,
they tried to make me crazy.
But I'm no victim.
I am me, and I'm honest.
Honestly...silence hurts worse.

I'm inside me beating on
my chest to get out—LOUDLY.
Can anybody
hear me? Screaming! Crying! LOUD.
LET ME OUT. FREE ME.

And I did. Truly.
Silence, my worst enemy,
did not defeat me.

"Yeah sis. You may slip, you may fall…but none of us are going to let you stay there."

— Taylur Holland

| On Wisdom |

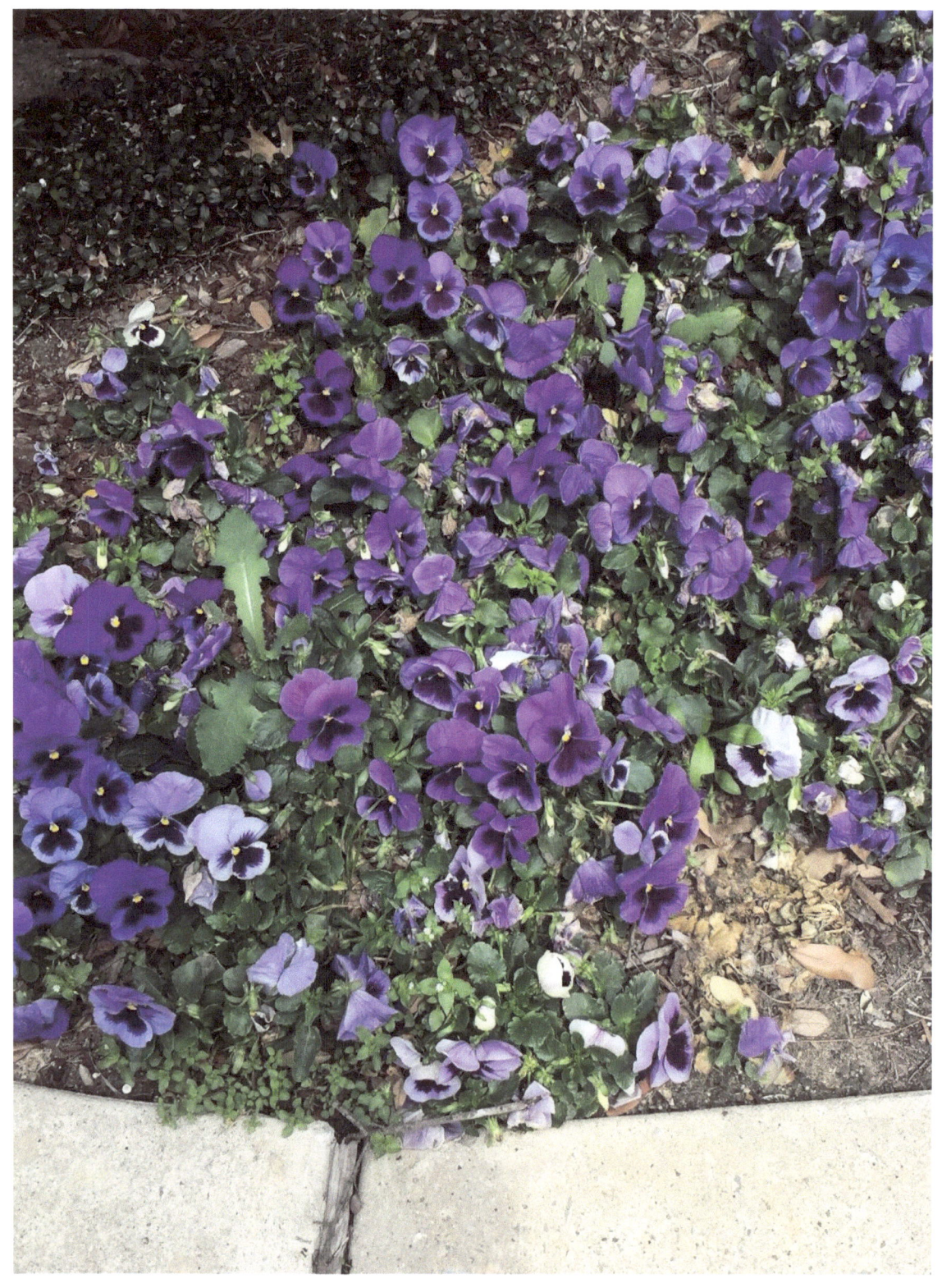

| Angel C. Dye |

" Your situation does not define you. Don't let it eat you up. Situations are temporary. Change happens, and storms cannot last forever. It's universal law…change has to happen."

— Destiny Casson

March 5, 2015

Dear Journal,

This has been one of the hardest weeks I have ever had. You don't know confusion until your life seems to be falling to pieces and simultaneously moving exactly in the right direction all at once. My biggest goal besides finishing this book at the moment is graduating college on time next year, and this was the week that that seemed so out of reach that I could feel myself becoming okay with the idea that I might never hold a degree in my hands. Not only did I have a past due balance to the university so large that neither I nor my mom would be able to pay it off in a year's time, but I was also seven weeks into a fifteen-week semester and still not registered for a single class because of the back balance. I'd only been attending two courses, and one of the professors supports and encourages me so much because she has seen me struggling to pay my own way through school since my freshman year and not giving up on my call to be a writer, but the second professor didn't know me very well and was not as understanding.

On Tuesday I was awakened to a knock on my dorm door from my dorm manager. I was going to be evicted by Friday if I did not get registered for some courses. I could not register without paying at least ten percent of my past due balance, and I had no idea where that money would come from even though I was working part-time while trying to stay in school. To fast-forward, I cried more than anything from Tuesday to Friday, and I confided in a friend then visited her. She must have told our other friends because by Friday they'd put together enough money for me to register. I didn't get evicted over the weekend, but Monday morning I made the payment to school right away and still got locked out of my room. I had to jump through hoops to get registered for the one class the professor was willing to let me into this late into the semester with a good grade. So here I am in my third year of college, many credits shy of graduating on time, taking only one class, and still believing that I am right where I am supposed to be.

All in all, so many people helped me over these past few days. They made sure I ate and had a place to sleep and that I knew that stumbling blocks are not the same things as stop signs. They just mean that you are headed in the right direction. I heard someone say recently that "we all experience fear, but courage is moving fiercely through that fear." I feared that I would lose what I love and want most only to realize that I cannot lose that unless I set it down and refuse to pick it back up. I am not what happens to me. I am shaped only by my response to the things I cannot control. And I am choosing to believe…to hope…to be a writer, a scholar, an artist, an activist, and everything that I am afraid I am not good enough or strong enough to become.

—A

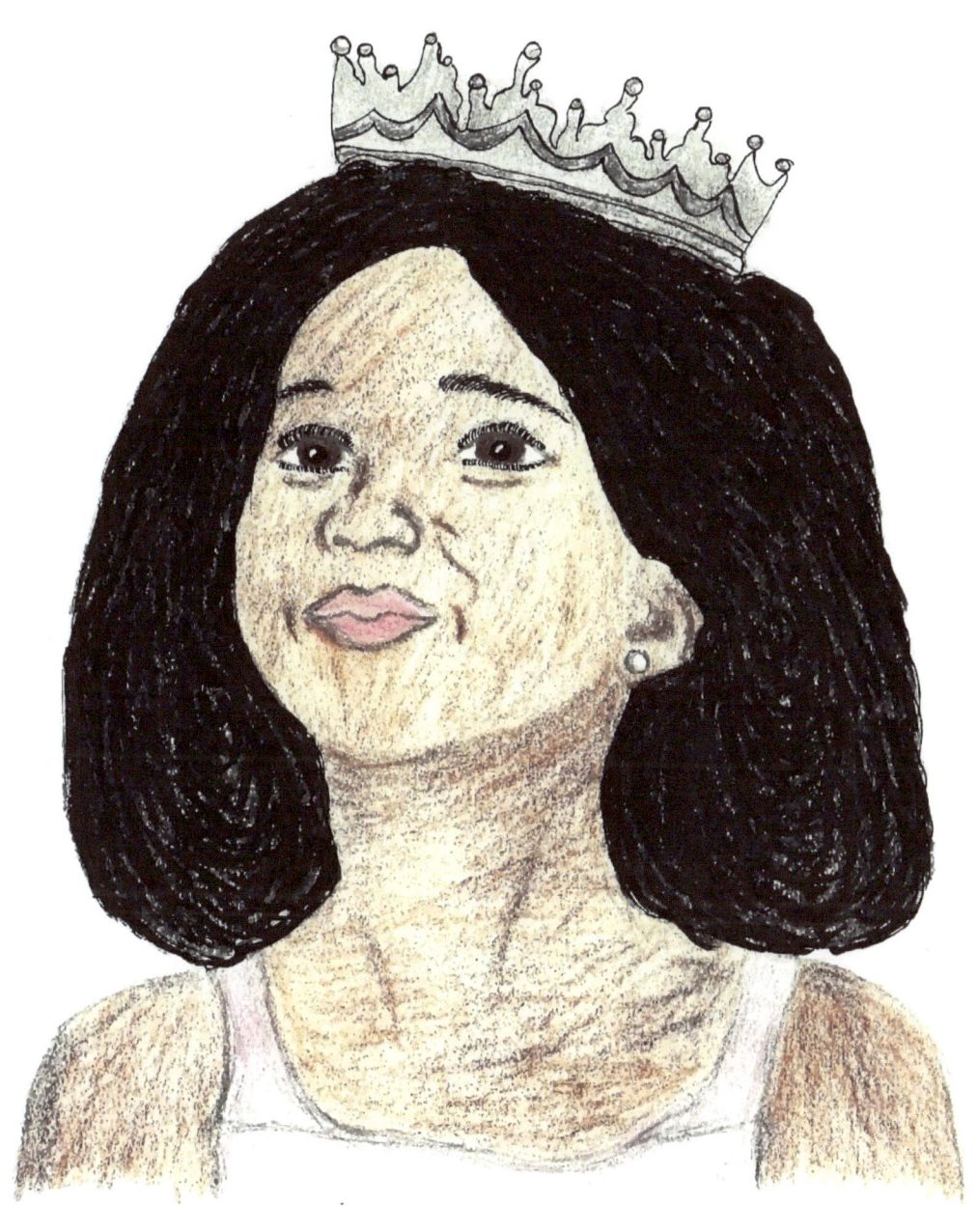

BABY GIRL, YOU'RE A *Queen.*

| Cyd Ahlberg |

Beautiful You Are | Queen Majeeda

Confidence
Self-acceptance
Integrity
A gracious personality
All these traits constitute genuine beauty
Still it has been said
Beauty is in the eye of the beholder
Therefore, each time you look in the mirror
You behold beauty
So embrace it!
And let no billboard, digital screen, television or magazine
Dictate what beauty is
Let no industry define beauty for you
For their ideals change from time to time
You are beautiful because you are!
With your coily hair texture
Earthen skin color
And God-made figure!
Embrace what you possess
That loveable face
And smile at your reflection
Beautiful you are
Such a sight to behold!
Striking
As the golden sun
Alluring
Like the scent of your favorite flower
As appealing as your favorite song
Stunning
Like the richest hue of your favorite color
Beautiful you are!
Now let no billboard, digital screen, television or magazine
Dictate how you feel
You beautiful queen
For there is no real beauty without
Confidence
Self-acceptance
Integrity
And your warm personality!

Don't Stop Dreaming | Janae Small

Put it in the universe
Or whisper it to an angel
Sprinkle it
Like fairy dust
Pour it over the earth
Bury it in soil
So that what you want may grow
Into what you see
The old folks say
Step out on faith

Honey, pick your head up

Get ready
Hold your hands out
Steady
To receive the blessing you asked for

Sugar, sit up straight

Plant your feet
Stay ready
Develop yourself
Know that you are wonderfully made
Say it in a prayer
Give it all to God
Know to whom you belong
To understand who you are
Write it down
Plan
Speak
See

Sweetie, speak up

He's listening
Someone once told me

To be clear about what you want
Know your status
Be of use
Tell your sister
Tell the clouds
Tell a butterfly
Send it down a rainbow
Admit to yourself

You are
covered

Baby, put your shoulders down

You've got nothing to worry about
Just don't stop now
Whatever you do
DON'T
Stop dreaming

Why are you surprised?
This is what you asked for

ADVICE TO A TUMBLR FRIEND | Elmina Bell

If you ignore your feelings they will only grow. No one knows what healing you need except you. Don't resist yourself; let out the negative thoughts you have of yourself. Then ask yourself, "Even though I am not where I want to be, what can I do with what I have?" If you are alive you have strength, life, a heartbeat, and that is all you need to start healing yourself.

If you feel toxic behavior or energy take a break. Sleep. Dance, and let the vibration of your soul's energy flow through you. Do something that keeps you in a non-resistant state where feelings flow freely. Sometimes healing means taking a risk or making a mistake that will in turn guide your vision and tell you what to do in order to walk on a path of peace. Doing these things I have just said will help you know and understand yourself better When you don't know who you are, you don't know what you are capable of and become stuck in limited perceptions. You are infinite. Period. Always remember that.

It takes time, but if you truly desire peace and success you will get better soon because you attract what you are. You get what you put out sometimes. You may feel like you are going in circles and not getting better. It is an illusion, one that you have the power to break. You can never truly go backwards, just into a deeper understanding of yourself. You are closer to the healthy you than you were yesterday. Own your past no matter how shameful. Own the negative things you have said and done because sometime from now when you have progressed you will say "Wow…look how far I have come. Look how I was able to transform myself." You would not be able to do that if it were not for these bad experiences and disorders you are facing.

Believe it or not you are growing. You don't have to believe it yet. Just say it. Think it. Try everyday, and you will eventually. Patience and consistency are key. And your experiences, whether they are bad or good, whether you caused them or other people did, are there to shape you into a better person. They are there for proof that you can grow and be resilient. It is hard to be strong, and it's easy to pay more attention to your failures than your successes. But by not giving up completely, by choosing to live, you are already going in the right direction...and that's forward. That's healing.

Dearest You
The very person my words speak to
This is for you
Those who come from struggle
Who didn't know Dad
The folk who Mammy checks her man's phone more than
your homework
Yep, I wrote it
You've reached the page
Where things get real
Regardless your gender
You were predestined
To be greater
If my mere words inspire
Then your every consonant and vowel should revolt
Before they are spoke
Thought leader
Regardless if you were born of my womb
You were called
To be greater
Than a gender role
Or a job description
Or minimum wage
So when you are uncertain
What your worth is
Know this
You are greatness

— @iamsimplynay

A List For My Unborn Daughter... | Natasha Alston

1. You were made from a genuine, deep, unadulterated love. Never allow anyone to tell you anything different.

2. You are here for a reason.

3. Your gender does not define you. It is not a box that you have to live within.

4. You only have one vagina...take care of it.

5. Your body. Your rules. Your way. Or no way.

6. "No" is a complete sentence.

7. My mistakes are not yours.

8. Honor your ancestors. You are here because of them.

9. God lives within you.

10. There is no one else on the face of this Earth who will love you more than I, your mother, do.

Sista to Sista | Cyd Ahlberg

Our blood flows steady like the Nile
We are queens birthed from the Earth's soil
The Heavenly Father made us strong and fertile
In body, spirit, and mind alike
We belong to ourselves, no currency or covet prevail
From our wombs we deliver new generations
With our hands we construct new nations
We are the source; without us man is naught
Through slander and oppression we may falter
But recover and ascend like the ancient phoenix
Our smiles light the paths to many destinations
The purest of hearts, we love even when love is not due
We wear our blackness proudly
Dressed in the finest of fashions
We are envied, mocked, and misjudged
Though all the world looks up to us without knowing
The blueprint of all that exists
From the naps on our heads to the worn soles of our feet
Beautiful black woman, latch on to your sister
Spread our message from ear to ear
We are the reason that all succeeds
And forever will we reign supreme
Beautiful black woman, latch on to your sister
For we are the key to all man's future
BEAUTIFUL BLACK WOMAN, latch on to your sister
Let her know that she is worthy and loved
Beautiful black woman, LATCH on to your sister
Hold her close in your arms and never let her walk alone
Beautiful black woman, latch on to your SISTER
And forever will our family grow

Dear _____,

Today I write to you! I choose to take this moment to address you and illustrate the importance of you living as yourself—for who you are and not what your parents, peers, or society dictate to you. Your subtle changes in hue do not imply your status in life. They do not stress your level of value within this world even though you are made to believe otherwise. God makes no mistakes; therefore, you are who you are meant to be. The judgment and lack of self-awareness infects your mind and destroys your spirit with every harsh word spoken in relation to your skin tone. The lighter you are the brighter you are, the more brightly you shine, the more you are deemed as the epitome of perfection. This is the lie that is fed to us all regardless of our race. The sad thing is we choose to believe it. Why do you not believe that the tightness of your coils and your full lips are just as beautiful? What is it that makes you less than you? The content of your character is what defines you.

The racial lines have become so blurred that you now walk through a fog of misunderstandings and ignorance. Years of your life have been lost through translation, maybe not through fault of your own. However, the uncertainty of changing your mindset has allowed you to conform to the negative connotations attached to the pigmentation of your skin. The tears you cry reflect not only your hurt but the hurt of those women who came before you—the hatred that has been inherited from one generation to the next. Release the ties of mental bondage which ignite the devaluation of beauty from our ancestors' experiences. Instead of being consumed with the mass media and latest trends of the latest celebrities, aspire to excel towards a state of self-acceptance, self-love, and self-discovery. Unlock your worth and become familiar with the notion of you not being defined by your appearance in racial hue. Find the new within the familiar.

When I look at you I see the warmest of smiles, the most intriguing features, the flawless glimmer of hope in your eyes. I see the strength of your body in every curve and the vulnerability with each strand of hair on your body. I see the confidence in your stride as you sashay past me. I see the beauty that you fail to see because you do not take the time to appreciate what makes you you. Society will continue to pigeonhole you and segregate you from yourself. Uprooting you from your connection with yourself. If you do not accept you why expect others to?

The bonds of sisterhood are now flimsy from the clear division of light and dark—when really we are one in the same. Women of color. Embrace one another wholeheartedly. Break down the walls of prejudice and rebuild a garden of understanding, acceptance, and empowerment. Do not let one another fall short. Do not tear each other down. Educate each other. Educate the next generation of beautiful girls and bless them with the power of knowing how to value what the world says are their flaws. They are the ones who depend on you to set the bar. To categorize one another in the aim of solidifying where you fit it is detrimental to you in the long run, having a devastating domino effect for those who will come after you.

Live the life you have as opposed to living the life that your surroundings stress that you must live.

Be courageous. Be bold. Be smart. Be wise. Be happy. Be aware. Be confident. Be successful. Be involved. Be understanding. Be creative. Be outstanding. Be brave. Be vibrant. Be colorful. Be individual. Be humorous. Be magic. Be graceful. Be educated. Be illuminated. Be beautiful. Be love. Be you.

Love,

Me xxx

— Nadine Robinson

Storytelling | A Conversation Between Sister-Friends – A & E

"I endured bullying and name-calling all throughout elementary, middle, and high school. In 8th grade I saw a commercial for a sperm bank. At this time all my friends were starting to get attention from guys and I wasn't, so I nonchalantly accepted that I would never have a boy love me or get married or have a boyfriend and that I would end up at a sperm bank one day.

I was afraid to tell my family and friends that I had self-esteem issues. I thought they would say, 'How can you think this about yourself?' It wasn't even that I thought these things about myself. They were just a part of my reality, and I'm a logical person. That was how I came to that conclusion in 8th grade about the sperm bank.

In high school I saw a friend attempt suicide and struggle with self-harm. That was the beginning of me always being the one there to help other people.

My junior year of high school I stopped looking in the mirror. I prayed everyday, but I never asked God to stop the name-calling because I felt like going to Him about these issues was me showing lack of appreciation for the way that He made me.

My freshman year of college I stayed in my room. I don't like parties, but that's not why I didn't go. I was legitimately afraid of what people might say to me or about me. I was afraid of the cycle repeating that I had experienced in elementary, middle, and high school. It was the first time I ever had panic attacks and anxiety.

That year I fell for a boy who was not willing to be serious about me or to even care for me just because I was looking for a father/friend/boyfriend in him. Throughout high school it was other people who had done things to me, but this time I had done it to myself.

It's cliché, but experience is the best teacher. You have to learn. It takes falling down and facing yourself in order to get back up and rebuild."

Dear Young Queen,

Some things in life are inevitable. No matter how much the people you love try to protect you there are situations you will have to go through on your own so that you can grow and learn. Unfortunately, heartbreak is one of those things. It doesn't matter if you are 16, 26, or 36; heartbreak hurts at every age. The first time your heart is broken will be one of the roughest times of your life. You will feel like your world is falling apart. You will find yourself questioning your worth and blaming yourself. You will try to figure out what you could have done differently. You might feel like you are all alone and have no one to turn to. You will think that you can't go on without this person. You will think about them all the time. Everything will remind you of them. Literally *everything*. You will think about them all day, everyday.

But then something magical will happen. You will wake up one morning and they won't be the first thing you think about. You might still think about them throughout the day, but now it's getting easier to focus on other things. Then one day you won't think about them at all unless you see something that reminds you of them. You might still get sad when you think of them, but now it doesn't take you as long to deal with the fact that it's over. Then one day you will hear a song that at one point made you smile because you thought of him—and then it made you cry because you thought of him—and now you can smile again because you realize that it's all just a memory now.

All of this takes time. These phases will come and go, and for the most part you won't even realize you're over him until you just are. The first time you see him again you might feel confused. Old feelings might try to come back, but stay strong. **The past is a great place to visit but you can never go to back to live there.** There's nothing wrong with reminiscing but remember that things will never be the same. You will never be the same, and that's not always a bad thing. But I beg you, don't let this make your heart dark and cold. Don't let this destroy you. Take this as the lesson it is, rise up, and be the queen you were born to be. Your king is coming. Just give him time.

From one queen to another,

Nadia Sims

Pearls for My Girl | Faith Esene

If I have a little girl I'll sit her down on my lap
while the sun blankets us in its warmth
and as she buries her face in my shirt, I'll whisper these words
Now child, if they say you run like a girl…
that means you run with all your might, and don't stop until you reach the finish line
If they say you fight like a girl,
that means you punch and kick until someone lands on the ground
If they say you walk like a girl…
that means you walk with your head held high
your eyes staring dead in the world's face and holding its gaze
 no matter how scary it looks

When my little girl grows a little older, we'll sit in the kitchen and sip tea
and I'll allow her to stand on my shoulders for a few minutes
look through the rusted window; peek into my past
I'll tell her that she is a beautiful mosaic worth keeping whole
That the broken shards are hard to glue back together once she's been shattered by those
prince charmings
I'll tell her that true love is
kind, not self-seeking, not deceitful
I'll tell her that she is not just hair, and eyes, and hips, and thighs
She is a brilliant mind, a warm smile, a generous heart
I'll tell her that patience is a virtue
and genuine love is worth the wait
I'll tell her not to toss her pearls to pigs

And when she becomes a woman
I'll tell her that motherhood is a sacrifice
That though she feels weak, she is strong
That the tears moistening her pillow and coming down like bullets
The blood spreading like red wine on the white bed sheets
The pain etched on her face
Will soon melt away when she cradles that squalling child

And long after I am gone, when her hair turns silver-gray like the moon
I hope she will remember all that I have told her
and let out a sigh of relief, knowing that she is not just a woman
But a queen

She | Barbara "Bobby" Rogers

The world is in need of a message today that says you are enough.
Just like you are, just like you were born,
before you add anything or take anything off, all by yourself you are enough.
Creations of the Creator we are, and what He starts He completes.
And who needs this message more than the women?
The gateways of life and the carriers of miracles.
There is a moment we leave God and join man, and to think physically within the
wombs of our mothers is where this miracle takes place.
It makes you wonder, how could they not know how amazing they are?
How could we not know?
Better yet, how dare we not know.
The beginning of creation
The likeness of God
The heir of royalty
The realm of existence
All of it right here in us
So walk like you carry the wonders of galaxies.
Dance like you start and stop the might of the sea with your hand.
Sing like your voice is the Sun's welcome to rise and set in the sky.
Love like you have the depth of a million oceans.
Live like the creation God crafted you as.
Fearfully, wonderfully made to change the world and bring life to it.
All these things are in you.
Be the wonder you were destined to be inevitably, when born as she.

My dear (insert your name here),

Life is a gift that you must not take for granted. It is a journey of learning and growing. Learn from your experiences. You will make mistakes, but don't be hard on yourself. Learn from your errors, and move along. Admit when you are wrong, and make amends if need be. Do not burden yourself with guilt but put negative situations behind you, and determine to be wiser as a result of them. No one is always right, and sometimes even our best intentions are no good and will hurt others.

There is an ancient proverb that says, "no matter how far you've gone down the wrong road, turn back." It is never too late to turn back, to start over, or to get out of a situation you realize is not meant for you. Never settle, never compromise, never sell your soul. This applies to various situations in life, be they personal or professional. Never be too proud to let friends know exactly what's going on, to let them know if life is not all you planned it to be. True friends will not mock you; they will be there for you.

Never be so desperate that you settle for less than you deserve. See yourself as essential and priceless like water, air, and sunlight. Let the thought of your existence evoke joy and happiness regardless of your circumstances; remember life is a gift. Dark days will disappear into bright sun-shiny ones. Be patient. Sometimes we have to make a concerted effort to change our circumstances. Be determined.

You may discover that there are certain decisions that only you can make. At times you may find yourself in situations that no matter how many people's opinions you get, you may have to choose contrary to what others suggest. Be true to your own conscience. Be firm in your resolve to make the most of what life offers you.

We all need a supportive, non-judgmental ear; find that trusted one. Be that trusted one for someone else too. Whenever it is possible to lighten someone's burden always offer a helping hand. We are divinely connected to each other. Honor that fact.

Finally, love yourself in order to love everyone else and love everyone as much as you love yourself.

With deepest love,

Karlene Hamilton
        a.k.a.
Queen Majeeda

Luna | Renée Walter

You must look to the moon when your mind's consumed with worry

or doubt or when no one answers the phone and all you need is someone to listen.

When you feel caged in and everything is dark, look to the moon.
I want you to look to the moon and remember
you can go anywhere or do anything you desire;
because despite how small the world may seem,
there are no such things as limits when it comes to our dreams.

Girl Talk | Angel C. Dye

Girl, can I talk to you for a second?
You look a little frustrated, a little discouraged, so allow me to remind you just how much you are loved and respected.
You belong to a lineage of warriors, survivors, originals, game-changers, icons.
You come from a stock bred of visionaries, innovators, geniuses, creators.
Your kind gave birth to the universe and all its mysteries.
Now what does that say?
Your kind nurtured nebulae and planets, hung stars and shot comets then rested to nurse them all from her bosom—the Milky Way.
Yours is a congregation that built generations held together by much more than just blood relation but by the desire to fit fairly into man-made equations.
Do you hear what I'm saying?
I'm talking about you.
Girl, woman, goddess, princess, queen,
dream, bright beautiful thing.
Yours is a royal priesthood.
Your lineage has borne the joy of full wombs alongside the anguish of full tombs and still found a way to live on.
And it may seem like just a pretty picture I'm painting, but the victory chant of your predecessors is an ongoing poem.
A perpetual sonnet, a time-stamped haiku, a subtle soliloquy, and often just a monologue you must force the world to listen to.
But your kind have never been known to be quiet or just sit down and take it.
They speak up, they speak truth, and some way or another it seems they always make it.
So I'm telling you to remember whose you are.
God's gift to Himself, regal heirs to eternity, hand-crafted beautiful minds, spiritual souls, glorious bodies made for playing this very specific and necessary part.
You are one-fourth girl, three-fourths wonder, bathed in marvel and sweet like summer.
Quintessential. **U**ndeniable. **E**xalted. **E**volutionary. **N**ame.
Talk to yourself more than you listen to Nicki or Rih-Rih or Miley or Bey or Yeezy or Jay-Z or Breezy or mainstream anything because you are underground sound so powerful and so profound they haven't even discovered a radio wave fit to broadcast your ingenuity.

Remember that when you comb your hair, wear your makeup, polish your nails, and clothe your body…
"I am a girl/woman/impeccably made human being,
and nothing and no one can ever take that away from me."

Embrace the Unique: Notes to My Younger Self | Taylur Holland

The strength you carry is incomparable.
The power that you wield is matchless.
You were designed by the Most High God.
The gifts He gave you were fashioned just for you.
Life won't always make sense.
You won't understand why you can't be like everyone else,
but give it time.
Your uniqueness is your greatness.
It is the key the world needs to collide gracefully with Peace.
Daughter, recognize your beauty.
Recognize the hope that is inside of you longing to shine through every
smile you grace upon passersby.
Jesus has not forsaken you.
He is your Advocate and your Defense.
He is keeping and preparing you for a space and time that will blow even
your mind.
He will always be with you.
Daughter, cherish who you are.
Embrace your differences, for they are pieces that have been so perfectly
knit together to make you whole.
I love you.

Dear Daughters,

You hold the key of life in your hands, and as you travel along your journey realize you are not alone. Life is so precious; embrace every moment, and go confidently in the direction of YOUR dreams. God has created a path just for YOU, so don't get so caught up in what Kim, Jane, and Sue are doing. Be your best self—everyone else is already taken. Besides, God has provided you with the tools to carry out your vision; all you have to do is ask! Ask for wisdom, guidance, and discernment.

On your way to greatness, take someone with you! Don't be afraid to share what you've learned, grow with one another, and support one another. Develop Godly character, for it will take you much further in life than your talents ever will.

Trust me, I know things won't always be easy, but with God, anything is possible! Just stay focused on the promise and not the problem. Know that God is always building you, even when it seems like He's breaking you. In order to be an OVERCOMER you have to actually overcome something. If it wasn't for the struggle you wouldn't have strength. *"To be victorious you must find glory in the little things."*

You are BEAUTIFUL! You are LOVED! You are a QUEEN! You are resilient, kind, loyal, loving, and you were created to be great! Don't let anyone tell you otherwise. I believe in you and I declare joy, love, peace, and prosperity in your life, and may you be blessed abundantly!

With love,

Angela M. Riggs

@msangiexoxo

Monáe, Janelle. "Victorious." The Electric Lady. CD. Bad Boy/Wondaland. 2013.

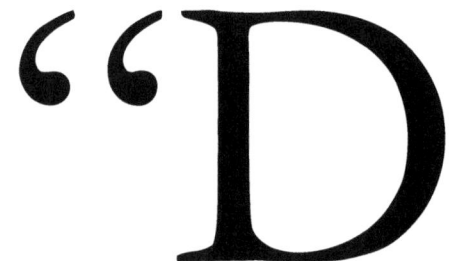"Don't be afraid to progress—even if you have to take a few steps back to do it. There will be some times in life when things take some twists, turns, and even reversals. Don't be afraid to progress, even if you have to take a few steps back to do it."

— Ms. RanaDee

Sankofa | from the Akan language of Ghana translating to "reach back and get it." Refers to a return to one's origins, culture, history, heritage, roots, and identity.

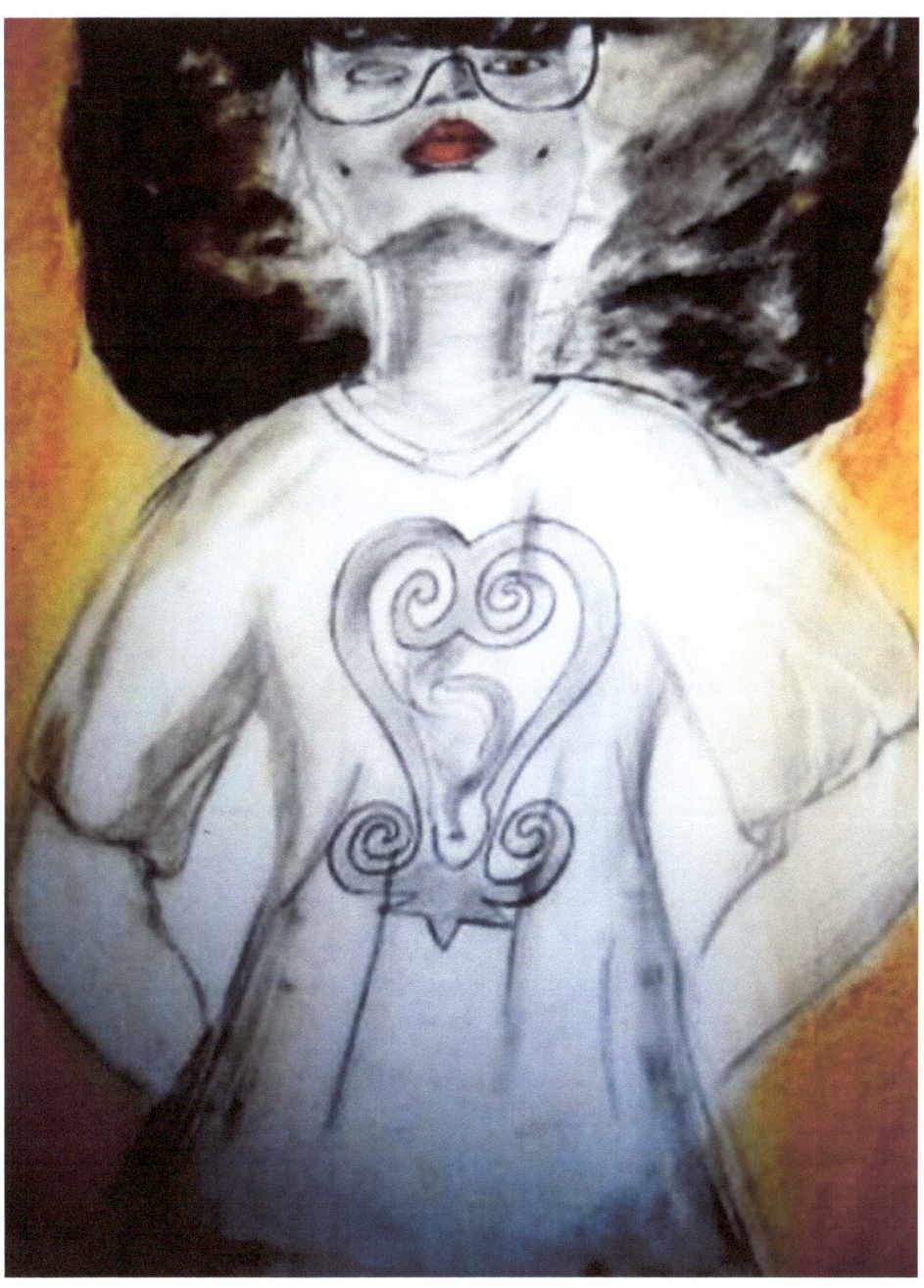

| Janae Hammond |

Back to Glory | Sadiyah Malcolm

The slave ship has sunken, but its ripples are ever-resonating,

and the effects thereof, stronger than we realize.

Our Black Kings turned into niggas, and our Queens: b—es and hoes.

The Black church was once a center of the Civil Rights movement, unity, and empowerment.

Now a source of business, a place of desperation and condemnation.

Once, the place we ran to, but now the place we run from.

But we're running through the streets looking for the next meal, the next high, the next baller, the next bad chick or the next nigga to pop off so we can retaliate.

Our babies mentally shackled

Pre-teens shakin', twerkin', and gyrating, teaching our princesses that rubber bands instead of wedding bands should make them dance.

Meanwhile the parents nod to the beat, and in doing so, perpetuate the cycle

Damn! Is there no cure for this Post Traumatic Slave Disorder?

It's as if the cycle continues without ceasing.

Indeed, the saga keeps movin' like a rolling stone and grows more vicious, more perverse with every revolution.

Brothas, I'm talking to you.

Black Kings and Princes, learn to respect your mothers, your sisters…

So when your Queen approaches your throne you can greet her, fully confident in the man you have become, well groomed, rooted in faith, the man just for her.

"Let not lustful desires take root in your hearts.

Lust not after her beauty in thine heart; neither let her take thee with her eyelids.

For by means of a whorish woman a man is brought to a piece of bread: and the adulteress will hunt for the precious life."

STDs and STIs come in pretty packages too.

Be strong, be loyal. And keep in mind that we're meant to procreate.

Your highest callings are to be husbands and fathers, protectors and providers, not baby daddies and absentee parents.

Love is not enough to build and maintain an empire, and love is a verb.

To my sistas

Black Queens and Princesses,

I love you so much.

I see aspects of myself in you all…from the emptiness felt in the heart of a stripper to the dignity resonating from Michelle Obama.

"Lift up your heads daughters, and the King of Glory shall come in. Who is this king of kings? The Lord strong and mighty."

Drop the influences and pressures of the world; don't drop that thun thun thun

Don't answer to b—es and hoes; answer to God and he will lead you to your king.

Be a modern day Proverbs 31 woman, a woman of virtue.

Exchange your booty shorts and miniskirts, and let strength and honor be your clothing

"Favor is deceitful, and beauty is vain: but a woman that fears the LORD, she shall be praised."

In closing,

"My people perish for a lack of knowledge…"

Brothas & Sistas, I pray you rise to your calling

"Know ye not that ye are gods, and all of you, children of the most high?"

Pursue divine alignment.

Reclaim your birthright, reclaim your divinity, reclaim your nature, and reclaim your roots

Be reborn

Family, reclaim yourselves

Arise, for your throne awaits you.

Ase! Ase! Ase!

Hotep

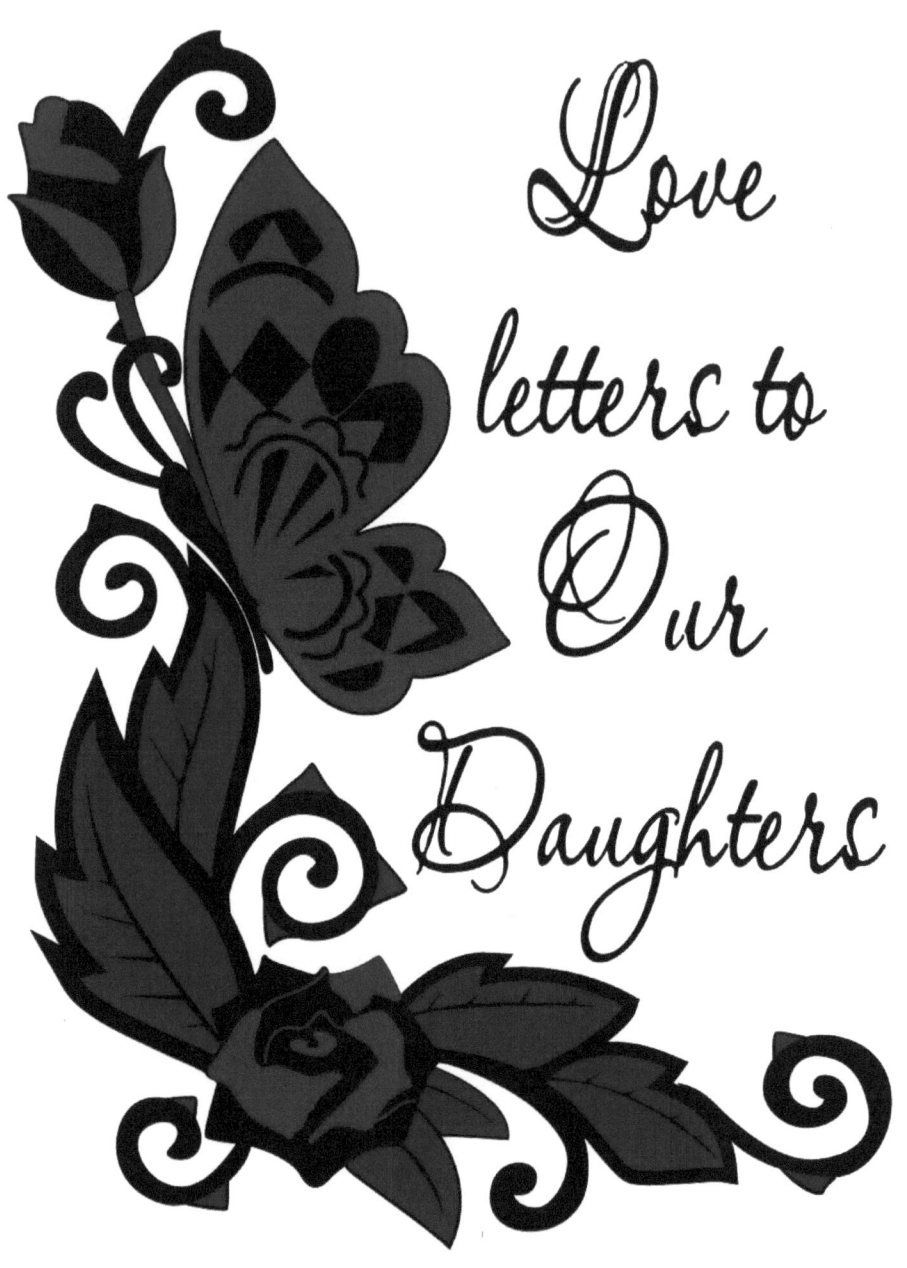

Love letters to Our Daughters

| RespectTheQueen |

RespectTheQueen.bigcartel.com

#LLTOD   #LLTOD   #LLTOD

#LLTOD   #LLTOD   #LLTOD

#LLTOD   #LLTOD   #LLTOD

#LLTOD   #LLTOD   #LLTOD

#LLTOD   #LLTOD   #LLTOD

#LLTOD   #LLTOD   #LLTOD

#LLTOD   #LLTOD   #LLTOD

#LLTOD   #LLTOD   #LLTOD

#LLTOD   #LLTOD   #LLTOD

#LLTOD   #LLTOD   #LLTOD

ABOUT THE EDITOR

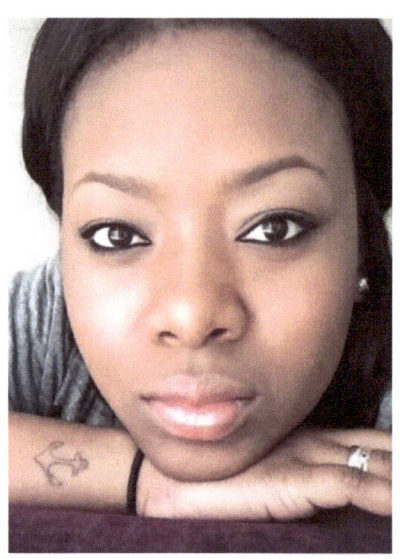

Angel C. Dye is a writer, poet, and spoken word artist originally from Dallas-Fort Worth, Texas by way of Milwaukee, Wisconsin. She is pursuing undergraduate studies in English and creative writing at Howard University in Washington, D.C. while beginning her professional writing career. This project is the second published work Angel has completed, the first being a collection of original poetry entitled *Rhyme Or Reason* which was released in August 2013. Angel hopes to go on to write more works and to eventually found a non-profit mentoring organization for K-12 students who want to cultivate gifts in fine arts. She believes that artistry and creativity are essential to survival.

www.ingramcontent.com/pod-product-compliance
Lightning Source LLC
Chambersburg PA
CBHW050723180526
45159CB00003B/1116